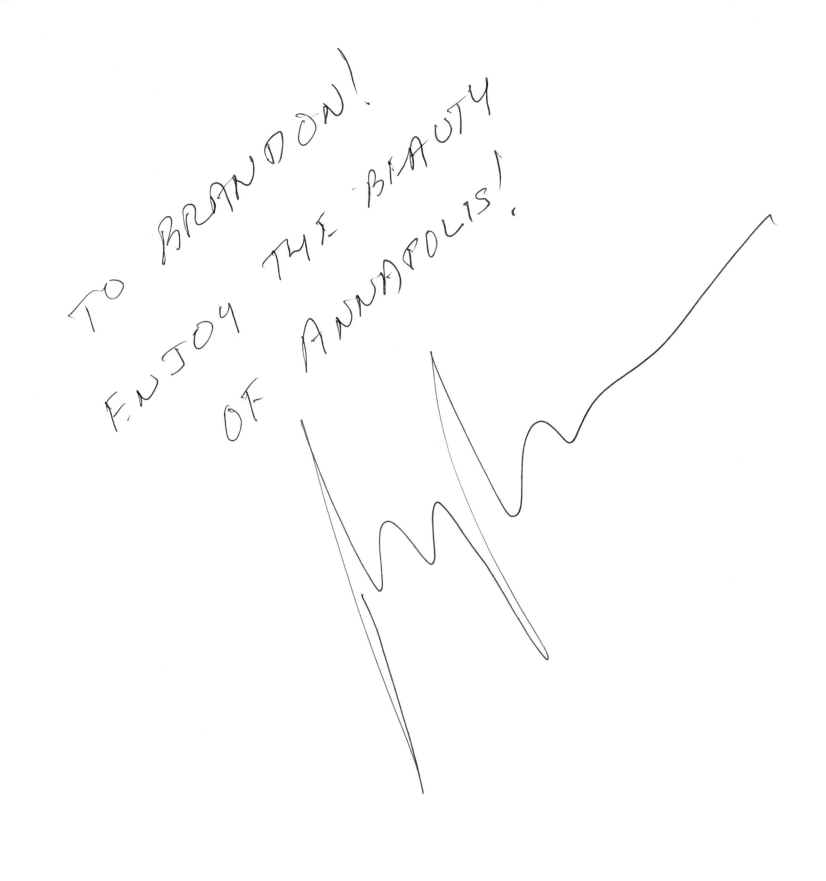

TO BRANDON!
ENJOY THE BEAUTY
OF ANNAPOLIS!

ANNAPOLIS
SAILING CAPITAL OF MARYLAND

WRITING BY
GINNY PEARCE

FOREWORD BY
GOVERNOR MARTIN O'MALLEY

PREFACE BY
GARY JOBSON

PHOTOGRAPHY BY
ROGER MILLER

COLOR GUARD AT THE UNITED STATES NAVAL ACADEMY

ROGER MILLER IN HIS STUDIO

image publishing, ltd.

1411 Hollins Street / Union Square
Baltimore, MD 21223-2417

TEL 410.566.1222   FAX 410.233.1241
WEB PAGE roger**miller**photo.com

DEDICATION

I dedicate this book to all of my friends. Life would not be the same without you!

ROGER MILLER, 06-30-09

ROGER MILER GENERAL THANKS

While I was photographing this book I was much like a lone, lost traveler stalking the streets of Annapolis looking for beautiful vistas at all times of the day and night. I was a hitchhiker on the water dependent on kind sailors to give me a ride. I was an honored "outsider" at the Naval Academy, Government House and the State House. I thank all the kind people of Annapolis for their help as I was shooting them, their houses and sailboats over the last couple of years.

ROGER MILLER, 06-30-09

SPECIAL THANKS

GOVERNOR MARTIN O'MALLEY for writing the foreword and keeping our state beautiful. Thanks to **JAY BAKER** and **CHRIS RIETH** at the governor's office for their help. **CARTER LIVELY** of the Hammond-Harwood house for his continued great advice on historic Annapolis. **JULIE CHRISTIAN** of the Upton Scott house and **JUDY KARDASH** of Acton Hall for allowing me to photograph their houses. **ROSEMARY HARTY** of St. John's College for assisting me in photographing the inside of St. John's College. **STEPHEN LAFFERTY,** Delegate of the Maryland House of Delegates, for helping me photograph the House and Senate while in session and getting me to the top of the State House. **MARSHA TRACEY,** Stephen Lafferty's legislative aide, and a good friend, for escorting me to the top of the State House and into the House and Senate. **SUSAN L. M. AUMANN,** Delegate of the Maryland House of Delegates, for her support of "The Arts" and maybe some poor photographers.

GARY JOBSON for his help with sailing and for writing the preface of this book. Gary you are not only a great supporter of sailing but also a great supporter of Annapolis. **DICK FRANYO** for letting me ride on his boat and helping me with sailing contacts. **GRIFF BELL** for giving me a boat of my own, for awhile anyway. **KEVIN MURPHY** for being a good friend and my boat captain in rough, as well as in calm water. **LEO S. MEHALIC** of the Naval Academy PAO and the Eastport Yacht Club for all his help and patience trying to explain sailing to me. Thanks also for taking me out on the bay to photograph the Melges International Races. **ED FREITAG** for allowing me to join him on his sail boat, *Downtime* during a sail race.

JACK REA a good friend and digital photography expert for all his support in keeping my cameras and printers working. **ROY SEWALL** a good friend, great photographer, and digital expert for all his help in getting me to finally become color managed. **JERRY STEPHANY** my photography teacher in college and still my mentor and advisor. Am I an artist? Well we are working on it. **TOM BECK,** Curator of Photography, at UMBC for being able to put words to what I do in my photography and for reminding me I have a long way to go.

ROGER MILLER, O6-30-09

SPECIAL THANKS

To everyone at the **MARYLAND HALL FOR THE CREATIVE ARTS**, the **ANNAPOLIS OPERA, INC.**, the **ANNAPOLIS SYMPHONY ORCHESTRA**, the **BALLET THEATRE OF MARYLAND** and **LIVE ARTS MARYLAND** thank you for letting me photograph their great work. We are all so lucky to have you in Annapolis.

A very special thanks to everyone at the **U.S. NAVAL ACADEMY** for allowing me access to all their sites and activities over the last couple of years. I would especially like to thank the following: **VICE ADMIRAL JEFFREY L. FOWLER,** Superintendent, for allowing me to do a new book on the USNA. **CAPTAIN MATTHEW L. KLUNDER,** Commandant Of Midshipmen, for all his assistance and for being at most of my photography sessions. **FREDERIC I. DAVIS, PH.D,** Associate Dean for Academic Affairs, for all his help with getting photographs of all the Academic departments at the USNA. **MICHAEL E. BRADY,** Strategic Communications Director, for his support of this project. **COMMANDER JOE CARPENTER,** Public Affairs Officer, for his help and assistance over the last year. **DEBORAH GOODE,** Media Relations Director, for being a good friend and guide to the USNA for more than twenty years. **JENNIFER ERICKSON,** Public Affairs Specialist, for all of her help in doing this book. **JUDY CAMPBELL,** Public Affairs Specialist, for all her help in doing this book. I also would like to thank all the **INSTRUCTORS AT THE USNA** who helped me photograph their classes. I would also like to thank all the **INSTRUCTORS IN PROFESSIONAL DEVELOPMENT** for assisting me photograph PROTRAMID and for getting me into Camp Lejeune, NC; NAS Oceana, NC; NAB Little Creek, NC; MCAS New River, NC; Mayport, FL and Kings Bay, GA. **JIM CHEEVERS,** Curator of the U. S. Naval Academy Museum, for reviewing the text of this book and always having the right facts.

ROGER MILLER, 06-30-09

CREDITS

Photography by **ROGER MILLER**

Design and Layout by **ROGER MILLER**

Foreword by **GOVERNOR MARTIN O'MALLEY**

Preface on Sailing by **GARY JOBSON**

Writing by **GINNY PEARCE**

Editing by **ROGER MILLER, PATTERSON KENNEDY, GINNY PEARCE**

Printed in China.

INFORMATION - COPYRIGHT

ORDERS

For direct orders please call or write for the specific pricing and the postage and handling to **IMAGE PUBLISHING, LTD.** at the above address. Discounts are available for stores, institutions and corporations, with minimum order requirements. You may also contact us for sales through our web page. The suggested retail price at the time of publication is **US$39.95.**

THE MARYLAND STATE HOUSE sits proudly beyond the beautiful flowers of spring. Construction began in 1772 on this, the third State House building on this site. It was expanded and improved in 1858, 1886, and 1902, and has become a lasting symbol of Annapolis.

IF YOU WOULD LIKE TO HAVE ANY OF THE PHOTOS IN THIS BOOK FOR YOUR HOME OR OFFICE THEY ARE ALL AVAILABLE IN PRINTS FROM 5" X 7" TO 8' X 16' FROM ROGER MILLER SEE rogermillerphoto.com.

SAILING ON THE CHESAPEAKE BAY Everything is great – good wind, nice waves, and the boat takes a port tack towards the next point in the race. Known as "rail meat," these members of the crew sit on the side of the boat and lean toward the water to keep the sails as straight up as possible. The crew works together and acts quickly to keep the boat on course. Life is just about perfect when you are racing a sailboat on the Bay.

CONTENTS

GOVERNOR MARTIN O'MALLEY is leading Maryland forward, even in the face of challenging times. A tireless advocate for Maryland's families, he has successfully fought for record investments in Maryland's #1 ranked, best-in-the-nation public schools, a strong safety-net to protect working families, landmark environmental policies, and public safety initiatives which helped produce historic reductions in homicides – all while restoring fiscal responsibility to state government. Prior to his election as Governor, Martin served seven years as Mayor of Baltimore. Born in 1963 to Tom and Barbara O'Malley, Martin was raised in Bethesda and Rockville. He and his wife Katie, a District Court Judge have four children, Grace, Tara, William and Jack.

FOREWORD
BY GOVERNOR MARTIN O'MALLEY

Annapolis is known today as the Capital of the great State of Maryland, seat of picturesque Anne Arundel County, home to the grand halls of the U.S. Naval Academy, and for many, as the 'Sailing Capital of Maryland.' From the brick-paved streets of our historic waterfront markets to the modern marketplace of our cutting-edge innovation economy, Annapolis is home to all of the diverse traits that make our One Maryland such a special place to live and visit.

In his Fourth, and most complete photographic history of Annapolis to date, Roger Miller tells us the modern tale of this ever-changing port town through the lens of his gifted camerawork. Annapolis retains its original design, with streets radiating out from the venerable Maryland State House, America's first peacetime capital, and the oldest state house still serving its original purpose – planning and shaping the future of the State of Maryland. It was here that George Washington resigned his commission as commander-in-chief of the Continental Army, and here that the Treaty of Paris was ratified to mark the end to the Revolutionary War and victory in the struggle for American Independence. Today, it is my honor and privilege to serve the people of Maryland from the same State House.

In its great 400-year history, Annapolis has continually reshaped and reinvented itself. The photographs on these pages capture the magical spirit of a city where our sport and leisure sailors walk side-by-side down Main Street with the men and women who proudly wear the 'Dress Whites' of the U.S. Naval Academy Midshipman.

One of the first to sail into this region, Captain John Smith, whose adventures and words inspired scores of colonists to arrive on these shores, had this to say when he first saw this land four centuries ago, "heaven and earth never agreed better to frame a place for man's habitation."

As you navigate your way through this collection of photographs by Roger Miller, I know that you will be struck by the beauty and heritage of our gateway to the Chesapeake Bay, and my home – Annapolis, Sailing Capital of Maryland.

Martin O'Malley
Governor

GARY JOBSON is a world class sailor who has won the America's Cup, many offshore races and one design championships. Gary is the author of 16 books on sailing, a commentator for ESPN and has won an Emmy for his Olympic coverage and an ACE Award for coverage of the America's Cup. He was inducted into the America's Cup Hall of Fame in 2003 and is an editor at large of *Sailing World* and *Cruising World* magazines. Jobson and his wife, Janice, live in Annapolis.

PREFACE ON SAILING

BY GARY JOBSON

I never tire of looking at sailboats. Yachts always look purposeful and yet at home on the water. Roger Miller has a keen eye for capturing images of boats as they perpetually navigate the precious waters of the Chesapeake Bay and Maryland's Sailing Capital - Annapolis.

A lone day sailor is just as interesting to observe as a fleet of racing yachts. There are many details to see. I like to look at the intensity of a crew's face as they steer, trim and work their boats for maximum gain. You can tell how fast a boat is moving by the foamy water being parted by the bow.

Every angle of a sailboat is of interest. Yacht designers work hard to create yachts that are sea kindly, fast, able to carry a full crew and stores, are comfortable to sit on and most importantly, pleasing to look at.

Classic yachts seem to get better looking with age and any yacht that sails swiftly is admired by all when the sleek craft passes by. It's no accident that sailors often wave at each other. This never happens in cars, trains or buses. Boats are different. When you leave land, a sense of freedom inspires crews to enjoy the surroundings. Every minute the scenery changes as you ply the waters of the Chesapeake.

Sailors have a deep respect for the environment, tend to be comfortable with advanced technology, and like to spend time with other sailors. As you look at the pictures selected by Roger, put yourself aboard each boat. Visualize what the crew is seeing and try to understand what they are thinking about at the moment a picture is snapped.

Some sailors study the sail trim to make the boat race faster than the competition. Others study the water, clouds, flags and competing boats to get an idea of how the next puff of wind will affect the boat. And there are sailors that just absorb the beauty. The wind in your face and the sounds of the water against the hull puts you in a peaceful state of mind.

Annapolis is a sailor's Mecca. The list of sailing icons is long starting with the U.S. Naval Academy, Annapolis Yacht Club, Severn Sailing Association, The Seafarers, the Eastport Yacht Club, and marinas, boatyards, working watercraft, and maritime businesses of all kinds. The town is over 300 years old. Sailors and the waterfront have defined this town since its founding.

Gary Jobson

AERIAL VIEW OF ANNAPOLIS The Historic District is in the foreground with Eastport across Spa Creek in the background. Beyond Eastport is Back Creek. At the center is the Maryland State House with the Governor's Mansion (Government House) in the front to the right. Behind the State House Main Street slants to the left and runs all the way down to Ego Alley and Spa Creek. The Naval Academy is top left at mouth of Spa Creek.

INTRODUCTION

Welcome to Annapolis!

Whether you arrive in Annapolis by boat or car, you will enjoy spectacular views of its miles of scenic waterfront. And, on a beautiful, sunny day you can't help but notice an array of small-to-large brightly-colored sails rising up from many of the boats out on the water. Catching the wind, the sails guide the boats out into the bay where experienced sailors and novices alike can enjoy a day of sailing. As the sun begins to set, the wind and the sails bring the boats back to the docks of a city, once a thriving commercial port, which has become known as the Sailing Capital of Maryland.

You may already have a sense that Annapolis is a unique city. As the capital of Maryland and the center of its government, Annapolis has a rich history dating back more than 400 years, and the promise of a future on the cutting edge of business, technology and architecture. As you take a journey through the pages of this book, you will see it all. The scenic photographs will take you through the streets where the early settlers once gathered. You can visit restored historic sites, explore miles of waterfront, then walk into modern-day Annapolis for cultural events or special activities.

Savoring each photograph, you will see Historic Annapolis – inside and out. Starting with the oldest working state house, you'll see where history was made and where modern-day decisions are put to a vote. From outside the dome to inside the dome, from the front steps to inside the chambers, the State House has become a lasting symbol of Annapolis. A tour of Government House will have you wanting more as you see rooms filled with antiques, portraits and furnishings that bring back different periods in Maryland's history. Then on to charming sites such as Paca House with its extensive gardens, St. John's College, St. Anne's Church, Hammond-Harwood House, streets lined with townhouses and streets where early settlers opened for business. Remnants of history have been left behind in these many historic buildings, houses, inns and taverns still standing today as a reminder of where we've been and how far we've come.

Annapolis is defined by its waterways – the Chesapeake Bay, the Severn River, Spa Creek, Back Creek and the other tributaries – with its tiny harbor as the focal point. Known as "Ego Alley," the narrow passage at the City Dock area is the place where boats cruise slowly by so their proud owners can show them off. The wide-open bay is a perfect place for sailing, boating, fishing or just about any water sport. Through these breath-taking photographs, you will witness the many boating and sailing events around Annapolis – from a distance and up so close you can feel the spray of the water and hear the wind shifting the sails. You'll see boat slips, boat shows, boats being built, boats racing, boats anchored for a rest, sail boats, power boats, big boats, small boats, yachts, canoes, kayaks, row boats, show boats and plenty of boat stuff.

Annapolis has always been a social place where sailors and "land-lubbers" alike gather for entertainment, to enjoy all types of cuisine and liquid refreshment. Whether you are a native of Annapolis, a temporary resident, a frequent visitor or someone here for the first time, there is much to see and do. The photos on these pages take you from the quaint inns and taverns of yesterday to the luxurious hotels and lounges that have become a part of Annapolis today.

There is an abundance of places to shop from shops filled with replicas of historic figures to the latest electronic devices, and from three-cornered hats worn by Revolutionary soldiers to the hip, trendy fashions of today. See the modernization of Annapolis in photos of the new Annapolis Towne Centre at Parole that transformed an old shopping plaza into a massive mix of condos, apartments, office space, and retail stores. See everthing from discount chains to exquisite shops, and restaurants from casual to upscale.

Established in 1845, the US Naval Academy is the premiere source of our nation's leaders in the Navy and Marine Corps. The photos of this state-of-the-art college take you beyond the usual tour. In addition to the many buildings, monuments, and statues that represent the history of the Naval Academy, you will see inside the classrooms where our future officers receive their academic training through a core curriculum and several electives. You'll see outside the Academy where Midshipmen travel to various locations to participate in drills and mock battles, fly aboard Navy aircraft, dive in nuclear submarines or cruise the world on Navy ships.

There's something for everyone in Annapolis. You can experience it all as you turn the pages of this book and enjoy photographs that capture the breath-taking beauty of Maryland's State Capital and the Sailing Capital of Maryland – Annapolis.

STATE HOUSE FROM EASTPORT All is quiet early in the morning on Spa Creek. Residents enjoy the peacefulness while they can. Soon sailboat owners and their crews will be preparing their boats for a day of sailing or racing on the Bay. The Dome of the State House stands majestically in the background above the trees.

HISTORIC ANNAPOLIS

Founded in 1649 by Puritans seeking religious freedom, the original settlement in this area was on Greenbury Point, on the north side of the Severn River and the western shore of the Chesapeake Bay. The remainder of the century saw waterfront development on the banks of the creeks in the present City Dock area. It became known as Anne Arundel Town and was a principal colonial port perfectly suited for the export of tobacco, which was the backbone of the colony's economy.

In 1694 Governor Francis Nicholson proclaimed the village as the capital of the English colony of Maryland because it was more centrally located – geographically and politically – than the colony's first capital, St. Mary's City. Shortly thereafter he renamed the town Annapolis, in honor of Princess Anne, who later became the Queen of England. Annapolis literally translates to "Anne's City."

Nicholson wasted no time in turning the modest town into an appropriate capital. Annapolis was designed around two stately circles. The construction of Maryland's first State House began immediately at the center of State Circle, not far from the harbor. It was completed in 1697. Just to the west, early planners laid out Church Circle as a home to the Church of England.

Annapolis flourished from the mid-1700's until the Revolution. Fortunes were won and lost on the race track just outside the city on what is now West Street. Annapolis was the site of the first parochial libraries and King William's School (now St. John's College). In spite of their close ties to London, Annapolitans enthusiastically supported the American Revolution. The passage of the Stamp Act in 1765 stirred the first patriotic tempers in Annapolis, and an angry mob ran a tax collector out of town. On October 15, 1774, the brigantine Peggy Stewart dropped anchor in the harbor carrying a load of highly-taxed, English tea. Ship owner Anthony Stewart sailed the doomed boat a bit further upriver and torched it. Annapolis had its own tea party.

There were no large battles on Maryland soil during the Revolution, though many troops passed through Annapolis. Among the most prominent wartime visitors was General Lafayette, who bivouacked here on his way to Yorktown in 1781. After the conclusion of the Revolution, Congress met briefly in the State House on December 23, 1783, when General George Washington resigned his commission as commander-in-chief of the Continental Army. Just weeks later, the Treaty of Paris was ratified, formally ending the Revolution. For a short period, between November, 1783 and August, 1784, Annapolis served as the capital of the United States.

The United States Naval Academy was founded in Annapolis in 1845 and spurred growth. The need for hotel rooms, taverns and restaurants resulted in a boom in the hospitality trade. Navy frigates, including the USS Constitution, were stationed here for midshipman training. A host of small sailboats drifted across the harbor daily as crews learned to sail.

Annapolis plodded through the Victorian years and early 20th Century, hosting dignitaries including Lord Mountbatten, Mark Twain and Woodrow Wilson who came to the Naval Academy. Old patriotic fervor bubbled whenever sailors were sent overseas – to the Spanish-American War in 1898, and then in the successive World Wars.

Little changed until 1952, when Historic Annapolis, Inc. was founded to preserve what remained. The group saved the important William Paca House from demolition in 1965 and has served as the city's architectural watchdog and purveyor of history and tours. The result is one of the most pristinely-restored early cities in America.

Downtown Annapolis is a registered National Historic Landmark with more than sixty 18th Century structures. Historic Annapolis, Inc. and a wide variety of touring companies coordinate presentations, organize tours of the City's outstanding historic homes, buildings, and waterways, and conduct on-going research into its past. Private and public galleries display collections of historical paintings, archeological exhibits, architectural ornamentation, and other civic reflections that recreate the history of Annapolis.

Annapolis is a relatively compact city with 7.2 square miles of land area along with 17 miles of waterfront on the Chesapeake Bay and its tributaries. It is conveniently located approximately 35 miles from both Washington, D.C. and Baltimore with excellent highway systems connecting Annapolis to both cities. Overnight visitors may choose from a wide variety of hotels, motels, historic inns, and bed and breakfast homes. Shopping is available in the Historic District and at several shopping centers and large regional malls.

One aspect of Annapolis life that never changes is the pilgrimage of lawmakers to the State Senate and House from January until April every year. Their chambers have grown and become modernized. But the issues are probably the same – taxes, road construction, schools, and fisheries. It's business in Annapolis, as usual.

THE MARYLAND STATE HOUSE dome rises above the trees on a crisp fall day with the American flag flying on top of the dome against a clear blue sky. The Maryland General Assembly meets in its Chambers in the State House every year for 90 calendar days, beginning on the second Wednesday in January. The governor, lieutenant governor, speaker of the House of Delegates and president of the Senate have offices here.

AERIAL VIEW OF ANNAPOLIS looking northwest at the **MARYLAND STATE HOUSE** which sits in the center of State Circle surrounded by Historic Annapolis. The Treasury Building sits in front with the House and Senate office buildings and the Governor's Mansion to the upper right. Main Street runs diagonally to the left.

THE STATE HOUSE From its grand staircase to the restored old House and Senate chamber where George Washington went before Congress to resign his commission as commander-in-chief of the Continental Army, and from the dome flanked by cherry blossoms to the 20th Century Annex of the State House surrounded by the lush green trees indicative of an Annapolis summer.

A view from the front entrance of the **STATE HOUSE** that faces the Annapolis harbor opens into the rotunda. This beautiful Rotunda is capped by the spectacular dome which still retains some of its original 18th century plasterwork. There are a number of commemorative plaques on the walls of the Rotunda.

THE MARYLAND HOUSE OF DELEGATES IN SESSION This is the larger of the two legislative chambers. The House has 141 members, three from each of the state's 47 districts. The Italian marble on the walls of both chambers is unusual with its rust and black coloring which approximates the gold and black of the Maryland state flag.

THE MARYLAND SENATE IN SESSION This chamber is decorated in red and white, the colors of the Crosslands, the red and white quarters of the flag which represent the first Lord Baltimore, George Calvert's, maternal family on the Maryland Flag. The Senate Chamber has two visitors' galleries which may be entered from the second floor. There are 47 senators, one from each of Maryland's legislative districts.

TOP LOOKING UP TO WHERE THE FLAGS FLY

STAIRS TO THE TOP OF THE DOME

TOP OF WOODEN DOME

STAIRS TO THE TOP OF THE DOME

There are 140 steps leading to the top of the **STATE HOUSE DOME**. Few people make that climb because it is not a part of the normal tour of the State House. It is the largest wooden dome in the United States and provides a great view of the historic area.

GOVERNMENT HOUSE FORM THE TOP OF THE DOME

A view of **GOVERNMENT HOUSE** from the top of the State House dome. More spectacular views of the State House show its distinctive dome against the sky – night and day. The beautiful Maryland State House is the oldest state capitol still in continuous legislative use and is the only state house to have ever served as the nation's capitol.

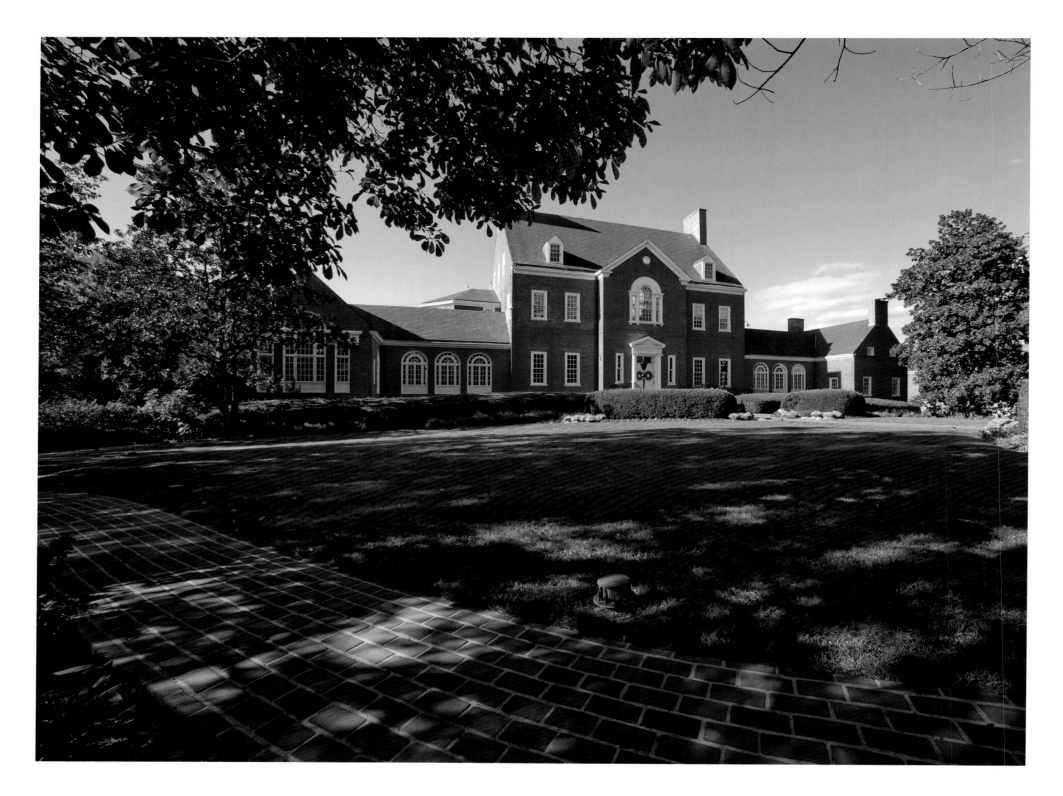

GOVERNMENT HOUSE–THE GOVERNOR'S MANSION has been the official residence of the governors of Maryland and their families since 1870. It is across the street from the State House and is where the governor entertains important visitors to Maryland. Each new Governor often makes changes to grounds, which are monitored 24-hours-a-day by the Maryland State Police.

The entrance hall of **GOVERNMENT HOUSE** features a large portrait of Queen Henrietta Maria, wife of England's King Charles I and in whose honor Maryland was named. Government House hosts art exhibitions from Maryland's art museums, private collections and the state archives.

There are seven public rooms in **GOVERNMENT HOUSE.** Above right is the drawing room with a painting of George Washington by Charles Willson Peale above the mantel. Government House is filled with antique and reproduction furnishings and paintings associated with different periods in Maryland's history.

The Federal Parlor of **GOVERNMENT HOUSE** features a mural of *Washington Resigning* by Joseph Sheppard. The staff of Government House keeps it humming as the center of the political and social life of Annapolis.

WILLIAM PACA HOUSE once engulfed by the Carvel Hall Hotel was completely restored by the Historic Annapolis Foundation. Careful examination of more than 20 layers of paint and wallpaper enabled the foundation to reproduce the original colors chosen by Paca when it restored the inside to its colonial-era splendor. Guided tours of the house are offered daily.

The restored **WILLIAM PACA GARDEN** is a wonderful example of urban garden design at the close of the colonial period. It features formal boxwoods and a lovely Chinese style bridge. The house and garden also offer a uniquely beautiful outdoor space for weddings and other special occasions, as well as an indoor meeting facility.

The **WILLIAM PACA GARDEN** changes with each season. You can take a self-paced tour of the garden at any time when the house is open to the public. The restoration of the Paca Garden is one of the great stories of historic Annapolis. The Carvel Hall Hotel was built in 1906 and was located squarely over the original garden. The demolition of the hotel in 1965 made way for the restoration of both the house and garden. Extensive archeological excavations, 18th century garden design books and the background detail in a painting of Paca by Charles Willson Peale provided the clues to bring the garden back to its present form.

WILLIAM PACA, one of Maryland's signatories to the Declaration of Independence, began building his stately brick home in 1763. He sold the house in 1780 and served as Maryland's governor from 1782 – 1785. The front of this historic Paca House (upper left) and several views of the garden from the terrace and areas inside the garden walls are seen above.

HAMMOND-HARWOOD HOUSE features what is considered "colonial America's most beautiful doorway." Ornate carved decorations by English craftsmen embellish this perfect classical entrance which beckons to the treasures within. The garden façade gracefully complements the peaceful green landscape created by noted colonial revival landscape architect Alden Hopkins.

HAMMOND-HARWOOD HOUSE exemplifies the very best of colonial architecture. Constructed in 1774 by Matthias Hammond, a wealthy planter, the house typifies the fashionable Palladian villa style favored by Annapolis' colonial elite. Built to plans of Oxford-born architect William Buckland, the house would eventually be owned by his descendants, the Harwood family. This colonial masterpiece is often proclaimed as the "Jewel of Annapolis."

ST. JOHN'S COLLEGE is the third oldest college in the United States. It is a liberal arts college with a unique curriculum based on the study of the "Great Books" of the western civilization. Each of the 400 students follows the same course of study, reading works of history, philosophy, literature, mathematics and science. An aerial view (top right). The tree seedling (lower right) of an ancient poplar tree planted on June 20, 1889 to commemorate the 100th anniversary of the college under the title St. John's College.

MCDOWELL HALL is at the center of St. John's campus (upper left). Due to St. John's proximity to the Naval Academy, the schools carry on a spirited rivalry seen in the annual croquet match (right) on the front lawn of St. John's. This match has been called "the purest intercollegiate athletic event in America." St. John's has won 22 out of the last 27 matches.

MCDOWELL HALL Despite its name, St. John's College has no religious affiliation. The school grants one bachelor's degree. Two master's degrees are currently available, one in Liberal Arts, a modified version of the undergraduate curriculum and a parallel course of studies in Eastern Classics.

ST. JOHN'S COLLEGE In addition to classrooms students have access to the dining hall, lounges, study areas, soundproof music practice rooms, an art gallery, and a music library. St. John's offers extensive intramural sports programs and extracurricular art courses. Major clubs and activities include student government, a newspaper, a yearbook, a film society, drama groups, a literary magazine and opportunities for community service.

BARRISTER HOUSE

ST. ANNE'S CHURCH

BARRISTER HOUSE

SHIPLAP HOUSE

BARRISTER HOUSE, built in 1723, is named for Charles Carroll, the Barrister, who was the longest living signer of the Declaration of Independence, dying at the age of 95. In 1955, the Historic Annapolis Foundation moved the house from its original location on Main Street to the campus of St. John's College. **SHIPLAP HOUSE**, built in 1715, has served as a tavern, a store, a cabinet-making shop and an artist's studio. Today it houses office and exhibit space for the Historic Annapolis Foundation.

ST. ANNE'S CHURCH is the third church to serve parishioners on this site since it was established in 1692 as one of 30 Church of England parishes in the colony. The present church was completed in 1859 in the Romanesque Revival style. It features a stone altar, walnut pulpit and pews as well as notable stained glass windows.

OGLE HALL

OGLE HALL

OGLE HALL

OGLE HALL

OGLE HALL is named for Governor Samuel Ogle, who lived here from 1747 – 1752. George Washington dined here on October 1, 1773 with Governor Ogle's son, Benjamin – an event noted in Washington's diary. In the century and a half that followed, a succession of prominent Annapolitans lived here. In 1945, it became the **U.S. NAVAL ACADEMY ALUMNI HALL** and can be rented for various occasions including wedding receptions, retirement parties, class reunions, VIP receptions, corporate events and meetings.

BRICE HOUSE

PEGGY STEWART HOUSE

SANDS HOUSE

RIDEOUT HOUSE

JAMES BRICE HOUSE was built by James Brice, who served as Mayor of Annapolis (1782-83 and 1787-88) and as acting Governor of Maryland in 1792. **PEGGY STEWART HOUSE** owner Anthony Stewart is noted for Annapolis' own "tea party." The **SANDS HOUSE** is believed to be the oldest surviving house in Annapolis. **RIDEOUT HOUSE** has been in the Rideout family since it was built by John Rideout shortly after his marriage to Mary Ogle in 1764.

WILLIAM BROWN HOUSE AT HISTORIC LONDON TOWN

WILLIAM BROWN HOUSE AT HISTORIC LONDON TOWN

HISTORIC LONDON TOWN

WILLIAM BROWN HOUSE AT HISTORIC LONDON TOWN

HISTORIC LONDON TOWN was once a thriving settlement on the banks of the South River below Annapolis. The **WILLIAM BROWN HOUSE**, a three-story inn dating back to 1760, is all that remains. It is surrounded by eight acres of woodland gardens where there is an extensive ongoing archeological investigation. London Town's success depended on the tobacco trade and the ferry crossing the South River. Both gradually declined in importance and by the early 19th Century the town had mostly disappeared.

BANNEKER-DOUGLASS MUSEUM

FREDERICK DOUGLASS HOUSE

BANNEKER-DOUGLASS MUSEUM

FREDERICK DOUGLASS HOUSE

BANNEKER-DOUGLASS MUSEUM A congregation of free African Americans built Mount Moriah Church in 1875 and worshipped here until 1973. In 1984, the Maryland Commission on African American History dedicated it as the state's official repository of African American culture with exhibits, photographs and artifacts. The **FREDERICK DOUGLASS HOUSE** built in 1895 was the summer home of Frederick Douglass and now houses collections that detail the history of Frederick Douglass and his family.

UPTON SCOTT HOUSE is one of the earliest grand Georgian homes in Annapolis. The house was built in 1764 by William Brown, builder and resident of the nearby London Town. He built the house for Dr. Upton Scott and his wife, Elizabeth Ross. Francis Scott Key, the great nephew of Elizabeth Ross, lived in the house while attending St. John's College. It is rumored that he later composed the final draft of the "Star Spangled Banner" in his upstairs bedroom.

UPTON SCOTT HOUSE, like many in Annapolis, holds its share of stories – some fact, some alleged. It is said that George Washington was a guest here, and many historians believe the house was part of the Underground Railroad, citing the tunnels under the basement which lead to Spa Creek as evidence. In 1872 the residence was acquired by the School Sisters of Notre Dame and used as a convent for ninety-four years. It became a private residence in 1968.

CHASE-LLOYD HOUSE

CHARLES CARROLL HOUSE AND ST. MARY'S

CHASE-LLOYD HOUSE

CHASE-LLOYD HOUSE

CHASE-LLOYD HOUSE A brash young lawyer named Samuel Chase began building his Annapolis home in 1769. Though his career eventually rewarded him as a signer of the Declaration of Independence, a chief judge and later as an associate Supreme Court justice, Chase ran out of money during construction. He sold the unfinished house to Colonel Edward Lloyd who hired William Buckland to complete his mansion. **CARROLL HOUSE** is the house of Charles Carroll of Carrollton, who was the wealthiest man in America and a signer of the Declaration of Independence. The house is on the grounds of St. Mary's church.

GREEN HOUSE

ACTON HALL

GREEN HOUSE

ACTON HALL

JONAS GREEN HOUSE is named after its owner, a printer's apprentice to Benjamin Franklin. Jonas and his bride moved here in May of 1738. Pieces of type, pottery shards and some samples of the Gazette paper printed by the family are on display in the house.
ACTON HALL The original land grant was given to Richard Acton in 1658 for a plantation and remained a working farm with large orchards well into the early 1900s.

The first sailboat race on the Chesapeake Bay likely happened the first time two vessels found themselves sailing next to one another and the competitive nature of sailors took it from there. The **CHESAPEAKE BAY YACHT RACING ASSOCIATION (CBYRA)** has documented the history of organized sailboat racing on the Bay back to 1908 with clubs organizing races, regattas and other events. CBYRA is an organization with a focus on educating new sailors, promoting boating safety and furthering the development of sailboat racing in general.

SAILING IN ANNAPOLIS

It has been said that that Annapolis is a "drinking" town with a "sailing problem." In the pages that follow, we will attempt to capture some of the joys of this "sailing problem." The real problem is that sailing is a seductive mental and physical challenge that bonds you with the wind and water. And, you must understand both wind and water if you want to win that race or if you just want to avoid having your sailboat towed back to port because you couldn't get the sails right.

We will add some cautionary notes here. Sailing can be a big problem if you decide to turn your small J-24 in for a larger more luxurious J-105 without checking with your investment broker, or if you spend too much time racing during the season and lose your job. Sailing is just one of those sports that gets you hooked. But, if you hang around long enough you will usually find a place in sailing that fits your budget and life style. In fact, you might find as many have, that sailing is "therapy" for modern-day stress.

Annapolis is uniquely located where sailing conditions are almost perfect. It is not too cold in the winter and there is not too much "fry your skin off" weather in the summer. Both the wind and tides are mild and fairly consistent. The Chesapeake Bay provides protection from rocky or dangerous shorelines and offers smoother sailing than the ocean. The Chesapeake Bay, the Severn River, Spa Creek, South River and the other area rivers and creeks offer plenty of places to sail and explore, wide-open spaces to race, several places to drop anchor, and a host of places to party after a sail.

To really understand the "sailing problem" you need to understand a bit about sailing and sail racing. It may look easy but it is amazing how complicated it is to move a boat with just the wind. There is a completely new language to learn – when you're facing the front of the boat or the bow, port is the left side and starboard is to the right. There's a mast and there are sails – the main sail, the spinnaker, and the jib, but you can't put them all up at once. The spinnaker goes up when you are "running" with the wind and then goes down when you sail into the wind and the jib goes up. You might wonder how you sail into the wind and get anywhere. You "tack" – sail on an angle to the right, which is a starboard tack, then sail to the left on a port tack – adjusting the sails as you go. You also need to know the "rules of the road." The sailboat on a starboard tack has the right of way and if you don't know that, you may have some angry sailors or cause an accident.

Confused? Take heart, there are plenty of people who will let you be a "pit bitch" and take the sails down and store them below deck. If you are not up to that you can always be "rail meat" and sit on the side of the boat with your legs over the side to counter balance the boat against the wind. If you are diligent, show up on time, and bring the right beer for after the sail you will figure everything else out in time and eventually understand reef points.

Sail racing is challenging and is controlled by a set of gunshots, horns and flags that you better understand or you will probably be disqualified before the race begins. You do not want to see a red protest flag before the race begins. Controlling these "conflagrations" and keeping track of all the tacks and jibs is not an easy job, but once you're hooked; you strive to do better and better with each race.

Thanks to a group of dedicated sailors at the Annapolis Yacht club and the Eastport Yacht Club, these races are well organized. During the season, Wednesday night races and weekend races are a part of Annapolis thanks to these very proficient race committees. Annapolis is also host to a whole series of national and world competitions such as the J-24 World Competition or the Melges 24 North American Competition.

Conflagration and sailing races of course do come to an end. After announcing the winners, eventually everyone seeks solace in port. Annapolis is well suited for this. Its safe harbor easily hosts hundreds of visiting boats, and the picturesque bars and restaurants of Eastport and historic Annapolis can put any flames out with an unending supply of food and drink.

When we say that Annapolis is a "drinking" town with a "sailing problem," maybe it is not a problem at all. Maybe it is just about perfect. Come sail with us.

The story of **J-BOATS** began with a $20,000 investment from brother Bob, and a speedy 24-foot sailboat that Rod Johnstone built in his garage in Stonington, Connecticut in 1975. Today, the J-24 has become the most popular recreational offshore keelboat in the world. In addition to the 5,400 J-24s that cruise the waves, there are more than 7,000 more J-Boats, ranging from the International J-22 to the J-65, that sailing enthusiasts have bought at prices ranging from $10,000 to $2 million.

J-BOATS are a big hit in the so-called racer/cruiser category: boats that perform well on the race course and are comfortable and easy enough for the family to day sail and cruise. Knowledgeable, experienced sailors often prefer the J-Boat. J-Boat owners have succeeded as champions of numerous offshore events in the U.S. and Europe.

Before the **START** it is important for the crew to develop a strategy for sailing the course by carefully monitoring the changes in wind direction and velocity and watching for variations in the current. The crew may also want to practice maneuvers and determine which end of the line is favored with respect to the conditions and competitors. Several minutes before the starting gun, there is a massive free-for-all where the boats are zigging and zagging around observing right-of-way rules until – BOOM – the race begins!

The **START** is the most important part of the race. A strong start can propel you into an untouchable position or at least give you a better shot at a top finish. A series of sounds and visual signals count the time down to the start. The goal is to be just behind the starting line at full speed just as the starting gun is fired. Not so easy – all the other boats in the race are all trying to do the same thing.

ENTERING A RACE. The races in Annapolis are run by many clubs, the most prominent being the Annapolis and Eastport Yacht Clubs. A "Notice of Race" explains the details of the race or regatta (a series of races scored together as a whole). It tells you who is organizing it, how much it costs to enter, when it starts, what type of boats can enter, when to register, and so on. After registering, you receive sailing instructions with rules and details of the race course.

PREPARING FOR A RACE Speed is one of the most important aspects of racing. Clever tactics and maneuvering better than your competitors are also important. Winning is much easier with a fast boat. Refining your equipment so that it is easy to sail and making sure your boat can handle the wind and the waves will help avoid the agony of a breakdown. Even little things like polishing your boat's bottom can make a difference in winning and losing.

THE RACE COURSE is set up so that sailors spend part of the race running with the wind and part of it sailing into the wind or "tacking." The members of the crew are well-prepared, so they know precisely when to adjust the sails to stay on course. Markers on signal boats along the way designate the course. The crews on each of the boats in the photos know when it is time let down the spinnaker and raise the jib or change the tack to maneuver the boat at just the right time.

RUNNING WITH THE WIND Sailing with the wind behind you is great. This forward motion reduces the wind and spray across the deck and you stay warmer. The special downwind sails are called spinnakers. If you let them all the way out, they help you go faster by catching more wind. The wind is simply pulling the boat along. It would be great to sail like that all the time. But, unless you are on a one-way trip, at some point you must sail back upwind.

ANNAPOLIS YACHT CLUB Anticipating the next sail, a fleet of keelboats sits at the Annapolis Yacht Club docks ready for owners and crews to embark on them for a cherished day on the water. The club has occupied this site since 1886. The newest clubhouse, in the background, is an oriental design built in 1962. AYC has been a leader in the sailing world and hosts world championship regattas and regional and local events. More than 2,000 members use the club as a home away from home.

ANNAPOLIS YACHT CLUB The Wednesday night race committee operates with practiced efficiency to start over a dozen classes for this weekly summer ritual. Just like a racing crew requires good team work to excel, the race committee must operate in harmony with the competitors, the weather, the racecourse and with each other. AYC has one of the best race committees in America.

THE CREW Although certain crew positions on some of the boats are more physically demanding than others, racing sailboats is for people of all ages and sizes and for both men and women. The most important characteristics of a good racer are concentration, quick reaction times, good analytical skills and a desire to learn. Men and women can compete equally well in sailing at all levels.

SAILBOAT RACING encourages sportsmanship because the sport is self-policing. Few competitions have on-the-water referees to enforce the right-of-way rules. Most race organizers rely on the competitor's sense of fairness. To win the race, members of the crew must let all of their senses work for them – from feeling the wind on their skin to reading the water for clues to the wind shifts.

WEDNESDAY NIGHT RACES Midweek racing at the Annapolis Yacht Club began in 1959. Races were not scored and prizes were not awarded. In the last 50 years, the event has turned from a nearly rules-free seafaring social event into a well-recognized series of races that attract about 1,000 sailors from all over the Chesapeake Bay, manning more than 100 boats in several classes.

WEDNESDAY NIGHT RACES Racers begin getting their boats ready in the afternoon and go into sequence for the first of six starts at 6:05 p.m. near the mouth of Spa Creek. The racing frenzy begins with the crews making sure they are looking at the right markers, shouting to each other and deciding which sail goes up to make just the right movement. The idea is to sail as fast as you can while looking around to see that you are going the right way.

61

SAILBOAT RACING can be anything from casual weekend or midweek racing to professional racing with television coverage and prize money. Sailboat racing has all the intensity of car racing without the noise, the burning rubber and the burning of fossil fuel. You're out in the middle of nature like an off-road racer, yet you're not tearing up the tundra. Once your boat passes, all you need to worry about is your wake.

SAILBOAT RACING Imagine a football game that takes place on the water, where the wind and the waves constantly change the playing field – that's sailboat racing. It's like a three-dimensional chess game where the board and the pieces are constantly moving. Racers must learn about the weather, the current, the hydro- and aerodynamics of the sails and the boat, and how to perform under pressure as a team.

The **WEDNESDAY NIGHT RACES** begin with a friendly attitude and end in a competitive frenzy for first place. Racers sail around several marks in the Bay then back into Spa Creek for the finish in front of the Club. The finish draws a large crowd inside the Club and on the nearby Spa Creek drawbridge.

Coming to the finish line at the **WEDNESDAY NIGHT RACES**. In an instant one boat is beaten to the finish line by only half a boat's length. It feels anticlimactic – but that is only because the best part is yet to come. After the boat has sidled up against the dock once more, the crews break out heaping plates of shrimp and lump crabmeat. Rum tonics and beer appear from below. The music starts up as the crew members dissect the race and catch up on the events in their lives.

THE EASTPORT YACHT CLUB will celebrate its 30th anniversary in 2010. Its active membership contributes to Annapolis' reputation as the sailing capital of Maryland. EYC hosts numerous regattas for local as well as international sailors with a passion for the sport. In addition to the waterside activities, EYC members have earned the reputation for throwing the best parties on the bay. The casual friendly nature of the club makes EYC a destination for reciprocal yachtsman from all over the world. Adjacent to the EYC is the **SEVERN SAILING ASSOCIATION** which is dedicated to one design competition.

The idea for **THE EASTPORT YACHT CLUB** was discussed as early as the 1970's. The actual organization was the result of informal Friday night social gatherings. Two hundred people were selected for the charter membership with no restrictions concerning race, creed, or sex only the proper love for yachting and the social activities of an active membership. The burgee pattern, the yacht club flag, was intended to represent the Eastport Bridge in an open position.

MELGES 24 is an America's Cup inspired one design sportboat introduced by Buddy Melges and designed by Reichel Pugh in 1993. Typically sailed with a crew of four, its comfortable and light-hull displacement design prefers to plane. Its 670 square-foot asymmetrical spinnaker lifts and pulls the boat forward on a downwind sprint. It adds speed, simplicity and ease of handling for a challenging tactical race. It is easy to rig, requiring only two sets of hands for quick set-up. It is light and easy to haul from race to race.

MELGES 24 NORTH AMERICAN CHAMPIONSHIP Organized by the Eastport Yacht Club, this is a one design series of races that attracts Melges crews from all over the world. Many high-profile yachting-based businesses line up to endorse, sponsor and support this premiere international regatta. The Annapolis area is a regular host to Melges events and provides ample facilities and social activities for sailors who come to race and enjoy the area's attractions

MELGES 24 With every Melges 24 sailboat produced and delivered there is a measurement certificate to match. All sailors need a valid measurement certificate to race. According to International Melges 24 Class Association rules, every owner and helmsman must also be a current class member. The International Melges 24 Class Association (IMCA) exists to manage the Melges 24 Class and protect the interests of Melges 24 owners worldwide.

The **MELGES 24** has a well established international racing circuit with classes at many of the most prestigious regattas as well as many stand alone Melges 24 events including annual National and World Championships, the venues for which vary each year. The Eastport Yacht Club and the Annapolis Yacht Club provide plenty of space to make Annapolis an attractive location for the events.

Early October brings the **U.S. SAILBOAT SHOW** to Annapolis. The notion that a floating show would be more successful, than a coliseum full of boats on platforms, was revolutionary when the first show took place in 1970. The following weekend the **U.S. POWERBOAT SHOW**, which had its debut in 1972 takes the same berths in the Annapolis and Eastport Harbors.

THE LARGEST BOAT SHOW IN THE WORLD features the hottest new racing and cruising boats from U.S. and foreign builders; smaller boats, dinghies, and inflatables; a vast array of sailing equipment, rigging and accessories; maintenance products and services and information on Cruising/Vacation Charters is available at the show.

GEMINI 105Mc CATAMARAN

TELSTAR 28 TRIMARAN

GEMINI 105Mc CATAMARAN

TELSTAR 28 TRIMARAN

PERFORMANCE CRUISING INC, located on Back Creek in Annapolis, manufactures the Gemini 105Mc Cruising Catamaran and Telstar 28 Trimaran. In business for 30 years, Performance Cruising has built more than 1,000 Gemini catamarans and nearly 100 of the Telstar trimarans. The Telstar length is 28' with an 18' beam that quickly folds to either 14' or 8' 6". The Telstar is trailerable and has a patented mast raising system. Described as a "pocket cruiser," the Telstar has full-standing headroom, four berths and a galley. She's capable of sailing at speeds just below 20 knots.

GEMINI 105Mc CATAMARAN

PERFORMANCE CRUISING INC The length of the Gemini is 34′ with a 14′ beam and is described as a "couples cruiser" for the Chesapeake and beyond. The boat is a practical and unique design. She has berths for up to eight, a forward-facing master cabin with a queen-sized bed, a cockpit that can be enclosed in screening or isinglass and a generous galley. The Gemini offers great sailing performance with lifting centerboards and rudders that enable good windward ability, yet the boat can sail in just 18″ of water.

CHESAPEAKE LIGHT CRAFT In a red brick building on George Ave., Chesapeake Light Craft has quietly cornered the market in an unusual maritime niche - the build - it - yourself wooden boat kit. Using sophisticated computerized machinery and old-world woodworking shops, CLC has shipped 20,000 kayaks, canoes, rowboats, and sailboats to 70 countries around the world. "Most customers are first - time boatbuilders," says owner John C. Harris, who designs many of the boats. Some opt to build their boat in CLC's classroom under the supervision of professional boatbuilders.

SOUTH RIVER BOAT RENTALS is nestled in Gingerville Creek on the scenic South River. We provide the boating enthusiast with powerboat and sailboat charters on the Chesapeake Bay. The company features fishing, wake boarding, tubing and sightseeing on its powerboat rentals. For those who prefer the sound of only the water and wind, while exploring the Bay, our sailing fleet is always a great choice for the experienced or novice sailor. Whether enjoying water sports or just taking in all the natural beauty the bay has to offer, it's always a great day on the Chesapeake Bay.

THOMAS POINT SHOAL LIGHT STATION is the most recognized lighthouse in Maryland. The current structure is a one and a half story hexagonal wooden cottage, equipped with a foghorn and light. The original stone lighthouse was constructed in 1825, replaced in 1838 and was finally destroyed by erosion. In 1873 Congress appropriated $35,000 for the construction of the screw-pile structure and its light which was activated in November 1875.

For boaters around Annapolis, the **THOMAS POINT SHOAL LIGHT STATION** is a symbol that you are almost home. In 1964 it was the last manned light in the Chesapeake Bay, and it was automated in 1986. It is currently the last unaltered screw-pile (stands on piles that are screwed into sandy or muddy sea or river bottoms) cottage-type lighthouse on its original foundation in the United States.

HISTORIC AREA

The historic area is at center Annapolis which is geographically defined as north of Spa Creek, east of the Severn River, south of College Creek and out West Street about a mile or so. Most of the historic sites of Annapolis are in this area. Some of the sites included are the State House, Government House, mansions, row houses and the Naval Academy. There are also great restaurants, hotels, quaint bed & breakfasts and just about any service you would need when visiting Annapolis. Almost everything in the historic area is within walking distance.

CONTEMPORARY ANNAPOLIS

The photographs in the following pages reflect the charm of historic Annapolis in a modern-day atmosphere and also take you beyond the historic district and the Naval Academy to other areas of Annapolis. Across Spa Creek, we'll explore Eastport, and take you further west all the way to the banks of the South River. We'll also travel east of the Severn River to explore some of the areas along Rt. 50 all the way to Sandy Point State Park and the Chesapeake Bay Bridge.

In exploring historic Annapolis, it's interesting to note that throughout the nineteenth century and well into the twentieth, Annapolis sat quietly on the shores of the Chesapeake Bay briefly coming to life during legislative sessions, only to sink again into a nine-month nap. Its mansions, small row houses, colonial warehouses, churches and academic halls never gave way to "progress," so that in 1952 when Historic Annapolis, Inc. turned its attention to preservation, it found an abundance of possibilities. Radiating uphill from the harbor to Church Circle are a hundred or more historic houses and buildings. All are now pristinely restored. Many of the buildings have withstood centuries of neglect and now project their history and its relevance in modern times.

Visitors flock to Annapolis, as they have for centuries, because of its rich history and abundance of activities, events, and entertainment. Many buildings serve the same purposes they always have. Restored historic inns welcome guests as they have since the Revolution. The kitchens at local taverns serve traditional fare to hungry visitors, while other restaurants now feature menus with French, Italian and even Mexican selections. In addition, many newer hotels and restaurants have sprung up in and around Annapolis providing modern accommodations and amenities.

Just across the Spa Creek you'll find the "Maritime Republic of Eastport," which has long been the local capital of the serious waterman and is the earthier, more diverse side of Annapolis. A visually eclectic area where million dollar waterfront residences bump up against boat yards and boat yard workers rub elbows with bankers and business people. It's Eastport's cohesiveness, built upon its diversity that makes it truly unique.

Eastport was settled in 1665 and remained farmland until the 1800s. The establishment of the United States Naval Academy in 1845 provided the catalyst for change. Eager to develop this area to house workers at the Academy, a building association constructed the first bridge over Spa Creek to Eastport. The peninsula has grown steadily since, and eventually was annexed by Annapolis in 1951. Laid-back is the word of the day in Eastport's cafes, taverns, restaurants and the many craft shops and galleries that dot the republic's streets. No matter who they are, what they do,

Eastporters – residents and business people alike – have a tradition of joining hands and working together for the benefit of this treasured community.

Further west of Eastport and historic Annapolis, you'll find more than 100,000 people living within a five-mile radius in nearly 40,000 homes ranging from large mansions to condominiums and from high-rise apartments to smaller houses and more boat slips and boats along the South River. Beautiful parks and recreation areas offer everything from picnic areas to a "doggie beach." This area also offers great cultural attractions with the Maryland Hall for the Arts, Annapolis's premier comprehensive arts center offering a variety of arts-related programs for people of all ages. As the home of the Annapolis Symphony Orchestra, the Annapolis Opera, the Ballet Theatre of Maryland and Live Arts Maryland, the area offers entertainment for every taste.

The Annapolis Towne Centre at Parole has completely revitalized the old Parole Shopping Center, originally built in the 1960s, and turned it into one of the premiere destinations where you can live, work, shop, dine and play. With luxury condominiums, apartments, hotels and commercial office space, this center also encompasses the foremost names in retail, fine dining and entertainment.

Enjoy a visit to the Renaissance Festival. Near Crownsville, this Faire will take you back to the days of knights in shining armor, jousting matches, fair maidens selling flowers, court jesters and other entertainers. From August to October, every year since 1977, weekends are filled with the excitement of a 16th Century English village in the days of Henry VIII.

East of the Severn River, along Rt. 50 is an area where traffic often jams during summer weekends as people in cars wait to cross the Chesapeake Bay Bridge on their way to Ocean City. It is also an area where there are many businesses, strip malls and outlet malls. Just before you cross the Bay Bridge, you can take a detour and enjoy the 786 acre Sandy Point State Park that offers swimming, fishing, crabbing, boating and windsurfing.

Enjoy a scenic view of the Naval Academy across the Severn River at the World War II Memorial on the east side of Annapolis. It's a great place to take your own photo, have a picnic or just stroll along the walls and remember those who fought for our country in World War II.

Contemporary Annapolis provides a mix of historic charm and modern-day convenience and offers something for everyone. Enjoy your photographic journey through this diverse and exciting part of Annapolis.

MAIN STREET AND MARKET PLACE AREA is where you will find, day and night, people shopping, talking, eating and walking. Some are dressed for a night on the town, some are in Naval Academy uniforms and some look like they just stepped off their sailboats and they probably did. This area is always busy for the simple reason that this is where you can find almost everything you want. The streets in this area are filled with restaurants and shops.

EGO ALLEY FROM MAIN STREET Looking out from the building at the corner of Main Street you can see the boats lined up on Ego Alley. This is a slightly cold evening in early spring and almost everyone is in the restaurants and bars staying warm. In the summer time this area is filled with people just enjoying its beauty. In spite of the modern-day atmosphere inside the shops and restaurants, the buildings still have a low key historic feeling.

The **CITY DOCK** area of Annapolis is sure to have people doing all sorts of things at just about any time of the day and most of the evening. Crowds of people move back and forth from shopping and dining to visiting to the Naval Academy and some of the historic sites of Annapolis. People stop just to watch the steady stream of boats negotiating up and down the narrow waterway which makes City Dock what it is. The boat owners want all to see their boats. A bride and groom celebrate their wedding with a ride up "Ego Alley."

THE NATIONAL SAILING HALL OF FAME & SAILING CENTER was established on Annapolis City Dock contiguous to the U.S. Naval Academy as a vibrant center to preserve America's sailing legacy and to engage sailing's next generation. The National Sailing Hall of Fame is a beacon of positive values, providing role models for outstanding achievement. It is an educational tool for teaching math, science, history and literature. It enhances stewardship of the environment and inspires all who visit to pursue their own highest aspirations.

85

PINKNEY, CORNHILL AND FLEET STREETS slope down from the State House to the City Dock. The narrow streets are lined with small townhouses, some only 10 feet wide. They have been pristinely restored and are painted in colors that reflect the colonial period. Some display markers awarded by the Historic Annapolis Foundation to identify buildings of architectural integrity, encourage restoration and preservation, and educate the public about the city's architectural heritage.

PINKNEY, CORNHILL AND FLEET STREETS are in the shadow of the State House. These older houses capture the charm of colonial times. Annapolis has a 350-year architectural history. Thanks to the preservation efforts, the entire downtown area was designated a National Historic Landmark in 1966. It is often difficult to park in this area, but once you are here, there are many things to do and see within walking distance.

MARYLAND AVENUE

WEST STREET

MARYLAND AVENUE AND WEST STREET are both lined with shops, restaurants, banks and other businesses. Maryland Avenue (formerly North East Street) was the first street in Annapolis to be paved—in 1867. Heading east from State Circle, it ends at Gate Three of the Naval Academy. West Street takes you to the west side of Annapolis where you will find beautiful recreational areas and modern shopping malls.

HOUSES around State Circle reflect a range of architectural styles and sizes. Historic Annapolis Foundation markers identify the distinct style and period using eight marker colors: Provincial Green – 17th-Century Vernacular, 1681-1708; Terra Cotta – 18th-Century Vernacular and/or Georgian, 1715-1800; Solid Bronze – Georgian, 1730-1800; Federal Blue – Federal, 1784-1840; Verdigris – Greek Revival, 1820-1860; Chesapeake Gray – 19th/20th-Century Annapolis Vernacular, 1837-1921; Aubergine – Victorian, 1869-1901 and Ochre – 20th-Century Distinctive, 1901-1938.

CUMBERLAND COURT

CUMBERLAND COURT

CUMBERLAND COURT is a small group of houses located behind the Hammond-Harwood House. Many people do not know that two of the houses on Cumberland Court were designed and built by a student of Frank Lloyd Wright.

The streets east of State Circle slope gently down to Spa Creek. Many of these spacious houses have large front porches, beautiful gardens and some spectacular views of the water.

BUDDY'S CRABS & RIBS is a family owned and operated restaurant, established in 1988, in Historic Downtown Annapolis. Enjoy a fabulous view overlooking the City Dock and Main Street with excellent food, service, and atmosphere. Choose from daily all-you-can-eat buffets and a full-service menu, including hard shell crabs, fresh seafood, baby back ribs, steaks, chicken, pasta, salads and sandwiches, kids menu and full bar. Buddy's is dedicated to serving "great food" with "great service" while having a "great time."

CHICK & RUTH'S DELLY, located in the heart of Historic Annapolis, is a tradition in Annapolis. Family owned by Ted and Beth Levitt, it is famous for more than just its sandwiches, subs, and old-fashioned milkshakes. Chick & Ruth's has hosted every governor of Maryland since 1967. Each morning Ted does the pledge to the flag to honor our service men and women. Whether it is breakfast, lunch or dinner, dining is always an adventure at Chick & Ruth's Delly.

RAMS HEAD ON STAGE, Annapolis' nationally recognized entertainment charm, is located on West Street in historic Annapolis. With more than 350 shows per year, top-notch entertainment is featured any day of the week. This intimate showcase features nationally known performers like Little Feat, Paula Poundstone, Phil Vassar, Chris Botti, Lyle Lovett, Blues Traveler, Neville Brothers and, as featured above, Kevin Costner's emerging band, Modern West. Call our box office or check the schedule online to see when your favorite artist is coming to town.

RAMS HEAD TAVERN first opened its doors in 1989 and was originally a tiny watering hole that seated up to 40 people in a brick-lined basement. More than 20 years later, the Meuhlhauser family has grown the West Street location to cover nearly an entire block in Annapolis, but the charm and cozy atmosphere still remains. The year round bier garden features blooming Wisteria in the spring; the dining room has a two-way fireplace while the brick-lined basement is a local favorite.

THE ANNAPOLIS INN, an elegant Bed & Breakfast at 144 Prince George Street was built by Mr. Thomas Rutland circa 1770. The house was sold to Dr. James Murray, physician to Thomas Jefferson during Jefferson's years in Annapolis. Several members of the Murray family were signers of the Declaration of Independence. The Murray family name was given to the Murray Hill Section of Annapolis. A tunnel of the Underground Railroad can still be seen in the cellar of the house.

FEDERAL HOUSE BAR & GRILLE is a great downtown destination for good food, good fun, and good nightlife. In an amazing historic brick building, Federal House is nestled among all the other great shops in town. Take your family for lunch or dinner and choose from a wide variety of traditional American fare with a focus on local seafood. After dark, you can enjoy fantastic live entertainment almost every night. Federal House has a large selection of draft beers.

97

GIBSON'S LODGINGS INN In 1681, this Annapolis property, now known as Gibson's Lodgings Inn, was assigned to the First Naval Officer of the Port of Annapolis, Richard Hill. The original structure, referred to in 1691 as "The Old Courthouse," burned to the ground. The existing 18th Century Georgian-style home was erected by Richard MacCubbin between 1760 and 1786. It was completely refurbished in 1905 and the facade of the "Patterson House" reflects the Victorian influence on Annapolis architecture.

O'CALLAGHAN ANNAPOLIS HOTEL Enjoy a warm Irish welcome at the O'Callaghan Annapolis Hotel, in the heart of the historic district, within walking distance of all the great attractions in Annapolis. All rooms in this boutique style hotel are decorated with furniture and fixtures custom made and imported from Europe. The John Barry Restaurant specializes in both Irish and local favorites - an amazing happy hour from 4-7 every day! Smaller Weddings and Meetings are our specialty. The relaxed and friendly atmosphere is what brings most visitors back!

99

LOEWS ANNAPOLIS HOTEL Imagine a place that provides passage to a centuries-old seaport village in a contemporary style. Loews is a place where views of Annapolis reveal a diverse cultural landscape full of historic treasures and uptown destinations. Inside, a tradition of excellence and service adds yet another level of contentment to every guest experience. Loews Hotel, centerpiece of the city, neighbor of the Chesapeake Bay is the source of countless memorable getaways. Set sail for freshly-furnished guestrooms to bring you rest and relaxation.

LOEWS ANNAPOLIS HOTEL Regatta-themed décor welcomes you aboard, and thoughtful amenities encourage you to linger. Business venture or family adventure, we put it all within reach. Launch plans at the city's most popular coordinates for business and social events. Where uncommon service accommodates gatherings of 10 or dinners for 750. A place where inventive interpretations of Chesapeake Bay fare are prepared for every meal in the award-winning Breeze Restaurant. Our nearby lounge, coffee shop and spa serve as beacons for further indulgence.

101

THE RESIDENCES AT PARK PLACE Just down the street from historic Annapolis and moments from the water, Park Place is a vibrant new community with a unique mix of luxury residences, retail, restaurants and office space. The centerpiece is the elegant residential building with a fountain courtyard and a charming, European ambience. Inside, the spacious homes welcome residents with gourmet kitchens and sophisticated finishes, including custom wide-plank hardwood floors, porcelain tiling and polished granite countertops. Some residences also feature private balconies and terraces.

THE RESIDENCES AT PARK PLACE Behind the stately façade, Park Place offers a wealth of amenities to make life easier and more enjoyable. Residents can take advantage of a fully equipped, private fitness center and pub-style clubroom. Outside, a swimming pool sparkles next to an expansive sundeck and a relaxing hot tub. And four-legged residents appreciate Bark Place, Park Place's very own dog park. Designed to offer a cosmopolitan lifestyle in a picturesque setting, Park Place has become a premier destination in Annapolis.

103

THE WESTIN ANNAPOLIS Situated in Annapolis' historic downtown district, the hotel is a short stroll to the Town Dock and Navy Football Stadium. This new hotel is the centerpiece of Park Place. Guests can get recharged in any of the 225 spacious rooms, all featuring the Heavenly bed and Heavenly bath, as well in the indoor pool and fitness center. This European-inspired hotel has more than 13,000 square feet of function space and has the largest ballroom in the city.

HOUSES ON SPA CREEK These houses in the historic area line up along the Spa Creek waterfront a little west of the Spa Creek Bridge. St. Mary's Church steeple can be seen rising in the background.   All is quiet on this spring weekday morning. Residents are busy going to work or getting things ready for the weekend. You can rest assured that in the evening and on the weekend Spa Creek will be alive with sailboats going out for a beautiful day of sailing on the Chesapeake Bay.

105

EASTPORT AREA

Eastport is to the west just across the Spa Creek from the historic area. Why it is called Eastport defies logic. It has long been the local capital of the serious waterman and is the earthier, more diverse side of Annapolis. Million dollar waterfront residences bump up against boat yards and smaller residences, making Eastport a cohesive community where boat yard workers rub elbows with bankers and business people.

EASTPORT Looking north toward the historic area from Eastport, you can see the Spa Creek Bridge on the left. The St. Mary's Church steeple rises above the trees in the center of the photo and the State House dome is to the right of it. The photo was taken in the early spring before the boat slips begin to fill with the many boats that have been in storage for the winter. The Annapolis Yacht Club is back and to the left of the red Water Taxi building.

HOUSES AND BOATS seem to vie for position in Eastport. This is on the south side of Spa Creek and the modern town homes are almost hidden by the boats in the foreground. Just about everything in Eastport is within walking distance, and nothing is too far from the water.

SMALL HOUSES AND LARGE BOATS define much of Eastport. With the establishment of the United States Naval Academy in 1845, many of the original houses were built to house workers at the Academy. Today many of these houses have been restored and are attractive residences for boat-owners.

THE BOATYARD BAR & GRILL is just a short walk over the drawbridge from City Dock on Restaurant Row in Annapolis' Historic Maritime District of Eastport. Its architecture and décor is part Chesapeake, part Key West and part Coast of Maine. It has been named by *Coastal Living, Yachting* and *Sail Magazine* as "One of The World's Top Sailing/Boaters Restaurants/Bars." At the same time, it has been named as the "Most Family-Friendly Restaurant in the County."

THE BOATYARD BAR & GRILL is open for breakfast, lunch and dinner – the Boatyard's Seafood Raw Bar is like none other in the area. Its "Film Boat and Crew" film the popular Wednesday night races and all sailing regattas and show the films nightly. The Boatyard is where local sailors, fishermen and all lovers of the Chesapeake Bay come to relax and enjoy pint drinks and great seafood. The Boatyard is committed to keeping the bay healthy, sailing fast, fishing with friends and making kids happy.

111

MARITIME REPUBLIC OF EASTPORT The peninsula has grown steadily since it was annexed by Annapolis in 1951. Laid-back is the word of the day in Eastport's houses, cafes, shops and galleries that dot the republic's streets. No matter who they are, what they do, Eastporters – residents and business people alike – have a tradition of joining hands and working together for the benefit of this treasured community.

LARGE HOUSES AND EVEN LARGER BOATS are found in some areas of Eastport. Many of these houses are similar to those found in Palm Beach or Cape Cod and these waterfront homes cover most of the land on which they are built. Large boats are tied to private slips just steps away from the back door.

WEST ANNAPOLIS

Further west of the historic area and Eastport, you'll find more than 100,000 people living in five-mile radius in nearly 40,000 homes ranging from large waterfront mansions to condominiums and from high-rise apartments to smaller houses. Many of the houses and recreational areas provide a view of the water and more boat slips and boats along the South River.

QUIET WATERS PARK is a beautiful park in West Annapolis. This photograph of the lake was shot with infrared as captured by Roger's specially - adapted camera. Infrared light is part of the invisible spectrum - you can feel its heat but you can't see it. When captured in film or now digital photography it creates a beautiful but mysterious image. Trees and vegetation turn white and the sky turns either red or blue.

QUIET WATERS PARK is located in West Annapolis nestled between the South River and Harness Creek. The park has 340 acres of hardwood forests and grassy fields with six miles of paved trails. There are some great views of the South River at the South River Promenade and the Scenic Overlook. The Blue Heron Center is available for weddings receptions or conferences.

MARYLAND HALL FOR THE CREATIVE ARTS is a multi-disciplinary arts center serving 100,000 people each year through high-quality, large-scale programs in arts education and the performing and visual arts. The 850-seat auditorium features performances by Maryland Hall and four Resident Companies—the Annapolis Chorale, Opera, Symphony and Ballet Theatre of Maryland. Arts education classes for all ages—from babies to seniors—are offered in disciplines such as drawing, painting, sculpting, drama, dance and crafts. Work by emerging and professional artists in all media are exhibited in galleries and exhibit spaces throughout the 1932 historic building.

117

ANNAPOLIS OPERA, now in its 36th season, is the professional opera company of Maryland's Capital City. It annually produces a series of opera aria concerts, a vocal competition, a children's opera, and one fully staged grand opera production at Maryland Hall for the Creative Arts. Annapolis Opera provides a venue for professional singers to hone their craft while giving audiences the opportunity to enjoy live opera performed by the opera stars of tomorrow.

THE ANNAPOLIS SYMPHONY ORCHESTRA has evolved into the largest performing arts organization in Maryland's capital city, currently under the artistic leadership of Music Director José-Luis Novo. Presenting Classic, Family and Pops Concerts, and special events each year, the ASO continues its mission to produce and present memorable symphonic music that increases the awareness, enjoyment and appreciation of music throughout the region.

BALLET THEATRE OF MARYLAND (BTM) is Maryland's premier professional ballet company. BTM ballet features classic American dance ideals - freedom, energy, athleticism, emotion - and portrays values and themes from American and Maryland literature and culture. BTM employs 12 professional dancers on full-time 30-week contracts, provides scholarships for 15 to 18 apprentice dancers each season and maintains a professional faculty of thirteen teachers in BTM's School of Classical and Contemporary Dance. It stages three complete ballets and one Rep performance per year.

LIVE ARTS MARYLAND is Annapolis' premier arts organization, performing and presenting a broad array of concerts and musical theater for every taste, from Broadway to Brahms. Now in its 36th year, this dynamic organization headed by Music Director J. Ernest Green is home to the Annapolis Chorale, Annapolis Chamber Orchestra, Annapolis Youth Chorus, the Broadway in Annapolis series, the St. Anne's Concert Series and music education programs for students of all ages, including the MusicWorks school partnership and apprentice program.

ANNE ARUNDEL MEDICAL CENTER The Clatanoff Pavilion, the center of Anne Arundel Medical Center's Women's and Children's Services, is a busy place. More than 5,700 babies are born here annually, making AAMC the second largest birth facility in Maryland. The Level IIIb Neonatal Intensive Care Unit (upper and lower right) is the highest-level NICU in the region. Many members of our remarkable team of NICU nurses have worked together for years, caring for more than 500 of our tiniest patients annually.

ANNE ARUNDEL MEDICAL CENTER has been a part of the Annapolis landscape since 1902, and is home to the region's leading experts in brain, cancer, heart and vascular, joint, spine and women's and children's health. The mission of AAMC's more than 2,800 employees is to enhance the health of the people they serve. Pictured above, the Acute Care Pavilion is the flagship of AAMC Medical Park, and houses the emergency department, surgical suites, private patient rooms and much more.

ANNAPOLIS TOWNE CENTRE AT PAROLE Thanks to a bold vision and unwavering commitment by developer Greenberg Gibbons to revitalize the old Parole Shopping Center, originally built in the 1960's, Annapolis now has one of the region's premier lifestyle destinations. This mixed-use masterpiece brings together the nation's foremost names in retail, fine dining, luxury residential homes and apartments and commercial office space.

ANNAPOLIS TOWNE CENTRE is one sensational destination where you can shop, dine, live, work and play. Stroll down Towne Centre Boulevard and feel the energy of bustling shops, restaurants and cafés. And take in the dramatic architecture, walking paths and eclectic crowd. With more than 50 fine stores and restaurants including P.F. Chang's, Gordon Biersch, Brio, Real Seafood and Chop House and Metro Diner you'll see why this destination puts you at "The Centre of It All."

125

YELLOWFIN STEAK & FISH HOUSE is located just south of Annapolis on the Scenic South River. With its panoramic sunset views, this restaurant offers a wide variety of seafood, fish, steaks, poultry and chops in a contemporary, upbeat, yet casual setting. Its famous Happy Hour and lively bar scene is a favorite spot for locals and Annapolitans alike. Looking for waterfront dining? Yellowfin Steak & Fish House offers the quintessential Annapolis dining experience.

SHERATON ANNAPOLIS HOTEL Thoughtfully appointed with a warm and inviting ambience, the Sheraton Annapolis Hotel offers travelers a home-away-from-home experience. When guests arrive at Sheraton Annapolis, they enter a welcoming environment where they don't just stay, but belong. It's a place where guests don't just come to, but come together to create memories. Experiences of interest in Historic Annapolis include the U.S. Naval Academy, and a plethora of dining and shopping options complement any trip.

Since 1977 the **MARYLAND RENAISSANCE FESTIVAL** has entertained hundreds of thousands of visitors annually in its 16th century English village visited by the Court of Henry VIII. More than 200 performers grace the streets and ten stages. Its 130 craft shops filled with many hand crafted wares, 42 food and beverage pavilions, 5 taverns, games of skill and attractions to amaze and amuse provide more than you can experience in a single day. Each weekend from late August through late October the festival is a cornucopia of fun, frivolity, merriment and mirth.

The **MARYLAND RENAISSANCE FESTIVAL** Knights from the jousting troop "The Freelancers" vie for honor on the field of combat and favor from the Court and the appreciation from the audience. The Freelancers parade at the Maryland Renaissance Festival before a crowd of more than 5,000 on the Field of Honor. The spectacle, held four times a day is a sporting competition with theatrical flourishes and staged combat to entertain travelers and take them back in time to the 16th century English village of Revel Grove.

The **MARYLAND RENAISSANCE FESTIVAL** During weekends every fall, bubble wand merchants play with patrons; Rose Jones (played by Melissa McGinley) hopes to sway King Henry VIII (Fred Nelson) as he weighs her case before the Royal Tribunal, an opportunity for nobility and peasants to plea before the King; a costumed customer joins in the mirth as a wizard and Shakespeare's Skum plies their fractured Shakespearean antics on the boards of the Globe theatre in the woods of Revel Grove.

The **MARYLAND RENAISSANCE FESTIVAL** A bevy of costumed customers enjoys the opportunity to meet, mingle and play in the village of Revel Grove at the thirty-second Annual Maryland Renaissance Festival. Over the course of nineteen days on nine weekends each autumn the forest and glen of Crownsville Maryland is transformed into a 16th century English Village. For a brief time each year the thirty acre village transports patrons to a magical time and place until the last cannon goes off and it's all history.

131

EAST ANNAPOLIS

After crossing the U. S. Naval Academy Bridge, you come into East Annapolis where you'll find the World War II Memorial at the top of the hill on Route 450 overlooking the Severn River and the U. S. Naval Academy. This monument to Marylanders who served in World War II is a rectangular amphitheater surrounded by columns and granite slabs inscribed with the names of 6,454 Marylanders who died in World War II. Stone panels and mosaic circles depict Maryland's role in the War.

SANDY POINT SHOAL LIGHTHOUSE is the second structure to hold that title. The current lighthouse was completed in October of 1883. It has gone through numerous upgrades over the years before it was automated in 1963. In 2006 it was auctioned off to a private owner for $250,000. It stands today as a welcome and guide to boaters going north or south along the bay.

CAROLINE'S CAKES Annapolis Baker Caroline Reutter has built an award-winning mail order bakery with time-honored family recipes for 7-Layer Caramel Cake and a number of other delights that define Southern Hospitality. Her classic Southern Desserts, rich in tradition and mouth-watering flavor, have built a huge following both in Annapolis and across the country via mail and web order. Located by the Chesapeake Bay Bridge, Caroline's Cakes is an easy and tasty stop for Annapolitans and beach-bound travelers alike.

CANTLER'S RIVERSIDE INN Don't miss the experience of cracking crabs at Cantler's The Cantler family fleet has been harvesting the Chesapeake for five wonderful generations. An Annapolis icon, Cantler's restaurant has been serving the area's freshest seafood to watermen, boaters and land lovers alike for 35 years. Sheltered in the quiet waters of Mill Creek and just minutes from the Annapolis City Dock, Cantler's prepares steamed crabs, clams, oysters, shrimp and fish - all served piping hot and ready to enjoy in an atmosphere reminiscent of Maryland's Chesapeake heritage.

135

JAGUAR LAND ROVER ANNAPOLIS is the Annapolis area's leading purveyor of luxury performance automobiles. Our goal is to preserve and enhance the area's rich heritage in everything we do; from the look and feel of our dealership to the many community events we support and sponsor. Experience the elegance, luxury and passion that is Jaguar and Land Rover. Located on Route 50 near the Severn River Bridge, we invite you to visit our showroom and discover elegance in motoring.

VISTA ON MILL CREEK This is one of the many great vistas looking out on Mill Creek. There are no crowds and all you hear are the birds above. This quiet serene beauty along the waters of small creeks and the Severn River is very much like most of East Annapolis.

CHESAPEAKE BAY BRIDGE is a dual-span bridge which connects Maryland's Western Shore at Sandy Point to the Eastern Shore at Kent Island. The first span was built in 1952 and is 4.3 miles long. A parallel span was added in 1973. The Bay Bridge, as it is most often called, is a major factor in the development of the Eastern Shore and the tourist traffic going to Ocean City and the Delaware shore.

SANDY POINT STATE PARK This beautiful 786-acre bay-side park offers a broad range of activities. Swimming is a must on a hot summer day. In addition to swimming, you can also try your hand at fishing, wind surfing, bird watching, boating, canoeing or kayaking. Or, you might enjoy a relaxing picnic or an invigorating game of beach volleyball. Since 1952, area residents and tourists have enjoyed this park at the foot of the Bay Bridge.

BANCROFT HALL On their way to noon formation, midshipmen march in front of Bancroft Hall which houses the entire brigade of midshipmen. The building also contains King Hall, where all of them are fed simultaneously three times daily, and Memorial Hall, where scrolls and plaques commemorate alumni and naval personnel lost in battle. Memorial Hall and the Rotunda of Bancroft Hall are open to the general public.

THE UNITED STATES NAVAL ACADEMY

More than a million visitors come to the Naval Academy each year for a guided tour around the grounds of this institution where many of our Navy and Marine officers receive four years of comprehensive training. The Department of Defense and the Department of the Navy invests its resources to the training of these young men and women.

The photos that follow will take you beyond the usual tour. In addition to the many buildings, monuments and statues that represent the history of the Academy, you will see inside the classrooms where our future officers receive state-of-the-art academic training through a core curriculum and several electives designed to qualify the midshipmen for practically any career field in the Navy or Marine Corps. You'll see beyond the Academy where midshipmen travel to various Naval and Marine bases for professional and leadership training and receive many hours of practical experience in naval operations. They participate in drills and mock battles, fly aboard Navy aircraft, dive in nuclear submarines or cruise the world on Navy ships.

Encouraging a sense of spirit and pride, the mission of the Naval Academy is: "To develop midshipmen morally, mentally and physically and to imbue them with the highest ideals of duty, honor and loyalty in order to graduate leaders who are dedicated to a career of naval service and have potential for future development in mind and character to assume the highest responsibilities of command, citizenship and government."

Each year more than a thousand plebes, first-year midshipmen, arrive in Annapolis to learn to live up to this mission. They face a summer that includes the strenuous physical training of boot camp and the discipline of military training which is part of the yearlong plebe development system. It requires them to stand on their own feet, to produce under pressure, to respond promptly and intelligently to orders, and to measure up to the highest standards of honor, courage and commitment. All Academy students are called midshipmen, which is a rank between chief warrant officer and ensign in the Navy. The discipline of each company, battalion and the brigade is managed by the midshipmen and supervised by naval officers. As midshipmen progress through the Academy, leadership responsibility grows and they assume more important roles in running their company, their battalion, and the entire brigade. They will someday be responsible for the priceless lives of many men and women and multi-million dollar equipment.

The Naval School was established by the Secretary of the Navy George Bancroft in 1845, with 50 midshipmen and seven professors on 10 acres of land. It became the U. S. Naval Academy in 1850 with a curriculum requiring midshipmen to study at the Academy for four years and train aboard ships each summer. As the U.S. Navy grew, the Academy expanded from 10 acres to 338 and from 50 midshipmen to a brigade of 4,300 today. In more than a century, the Navy has moved from a fleet of sail and steam-powered ships to a high-tech fleet of nuclear-powered submarines, surface ships and supersonic aircraft. The Academy continues to expand its training to prepare midshipmen for each new challenge.

The Naval Academy first accepted women as midshipmen in 1976 when Congress authorized the admission of women to all of the service academies. Women comprise more than 20 percent of entering plebes – or freshmen – and they pursue the same academic and professional training as their male classmates.

The athletic program and athletic teams at the Naval Academy are an integral part of the overall education and provide leadership opportunities and the experiences of team play, cooperation, commitment and sacrifice. The primary goal is fitness, which is vital for health, personal appearance and well-being.

Known as "The Yard," the Academy features a variety of architecture from Beaux Arts style to contemporary. The copper mansard roofs throughout tie the campus together. Bancroft Hall dates back to the early 1900s and is among the largest dormitories in the country, and the largest building at the Yard. It is home to the entire brigade of midshipmen. The dining hall accommodates all of them at once, chowing down on more than a thousand loaves of bread and more in one sitting.

The Chapel was built in 1904-1908 and dedicated in May 1908. Its copper dome is visible from well out into the Chesapeake Bay. The Yard has a vast array of monuments and bronze tablets recalling places where sailors and Marines fought and died. The Naval Academy Museum displays artifacts that represent the sacrifices of graduates from the Revolution through Desert Storm.

The Academy is open from 9 a.m. to 5 p.m. daily. You can take a guided tour with a commercial service in Annapolis or through the Academy's visitor center. Admissions presentations are held regularly and the Academy offers the opportunity for rising high school seniors to visit the Naval Academy for one week during the summer.

BANCROFT HALL Midshipmen walk along **STRIBLING WALK** to and from Bancroft Hall, among the largest dormitories in the world. It contains 1,700 rooms, 4.8 miles of corridors, and 33 acres of floor space. In addition to midshipmen rooms, Bancroft Hall houses offices for the Commandant of Midshipmen, six battalion officers, six battalion chaplains, 30 company officers and their senior enlisted leaders, a barbershop, bank, travel office, restaurant, bookstore, general store, laundromat, uniform store, cobbler, the band, a post office, a gymnasium, and full medical, dental, optometry and orthopedics clinics.

BANCROFT HALL WITH PLEBES LINED UP FOR CLASS PHOTO

ARCHITECTURAL DETAIL ON BANCROFT HALL

ARCHITECTURAL DETAIL ON BANCROFT HALL

BANCROFT HALL

BANCROFT HALL was completed in 1905 with additions in 1920, 1941 and 1961. Bancroft Hall was named for the Academy's founder, Secretary of the Navy George Bancroft, was designed by Architect Ernest Flagg (1857 – 1947) in the Beaux Arts style with a mansard roof. Used widely by French architect Nicolas Francois Mansart (1598 – 1666), the mansard roof makes maximum use of the interior space of the upper store or attic. The design also includes carvings of many decorative naval symbols such as the school's coat of arms and the bow of a ship.

143

MEMORIAL HALL

ROTUNDA OF BANCROFT HALL

ROTUNDA OF BANCROFT HALL

AERIAL OF NAVAL ACADEMY LOOKING SOUTHEAST

MEMORIAL HALL, which is inside Bancroft Hall, is one of the Academy's most hallowed places with memorabilia including a replica of the original battle flag bearing the words "Don't Give Up the Ship," used in 1813 during the battle of Lake Erie. The Rotunda with its marble floor is the main entrance to Bancroft Hall and a central meeting place. An aerial view of the Academy shows the Administration building to the left, the Chapel in the center and Buchanan House, the Superintendant's residence, to the right.

AN AERIAL VIEW OF THE NAVAL ACADEMY Looking northwest, the Severn River is on the right and the mouth of Spa Creek is to the left. Far left are the Visitor's Center and Halsey Field House. Along the water's edge are sports fields used for team practices and various sporting events. The large group of buildings in the center makes up Bancroft Hall. The Wesley Brown Field House and the Sailing Center sit to the right front with more sports fields to the far right.

145

U.S. NAVAL ACADEMY CHAPEL The most prominent building, aside from Bancroft Hall, is the Chapel which is centrally located on the highest ground in the Yard. Many refer to the Chapel as "The Cathedral of the Navy," due to its noble grandeur and monumental proportions. No matter how one approaches Annapolis, by land, sea, or air, its tiered dome dominates the skyline.

INTERIOR OF CHAPEL WITH PORTER WINDOW

INTERIOR OF THE CHAPEL LOOKING UP AT THE THE DOME

JOHN PAUL JONES CRYPT BENEATH THE CHAPEL

INTERIOR OF NAVAL ACADEMY CHAPEL

U.S. NAVAL CHAPEL As one enters the sanctuary, the eye is drawn to the famous stained glass Porter window. Made by Louis C. Tiffany Studios, it is a memorial to Admiral David Dixon Porter. The dome rises above the altar and adds magical lighting to the Chapel. In addition to regular services, the Chapel hosts many weddings, baptisms, funerals, and memorial services each year. The great naval leader of the American Revolution, Commodore John Paul Jones is entombed beneath the Chapel.

147

TECUMSEH BEING PAINTED

ZIMMERMAN BANDSTAND

TECUMSEH PAINTED FOR EVENT

BUCHANAN HOUSE

This heroic bust of a Native American carved as a figurehead of the *U.S.S. Delaware* was named **"TECUMSEH"** by the midshipmen who paint him at various times of the year. Tecumseh sports different colors during football season, graduation, and other celebrations. The **ZIMMERMAN GAZEBO BANDSTAND** in front of the Chapel was built in 1923 and named after Bandmaster Charles A. Zimmerman who composed a new piece of music for each graduating class. **BUCHANAN HOUSE** is the residence of the Superintendant.

MAHAN HALL

WESLEY BROWN FIELD HOUSE

INTERIOR OF MAHAN HALL

WESLEY BROWN FIELD HOUSE

MAHAN HALL is named after Rear Admiral Alfred Thayer Mahan, a naval strategist and historian. His book, *The Influence of Sea Power Upon History*, was recognized internationally and transformed naval strategy. Inside Mahan Hall, you will find a large theatre and classrooms. **WESLEY BROWN FIELD HOUSE** is a 140,000 square-foot state-of-the-art athletic facility that is named after the first African-American who graduated from the Naval Academy in 1949.

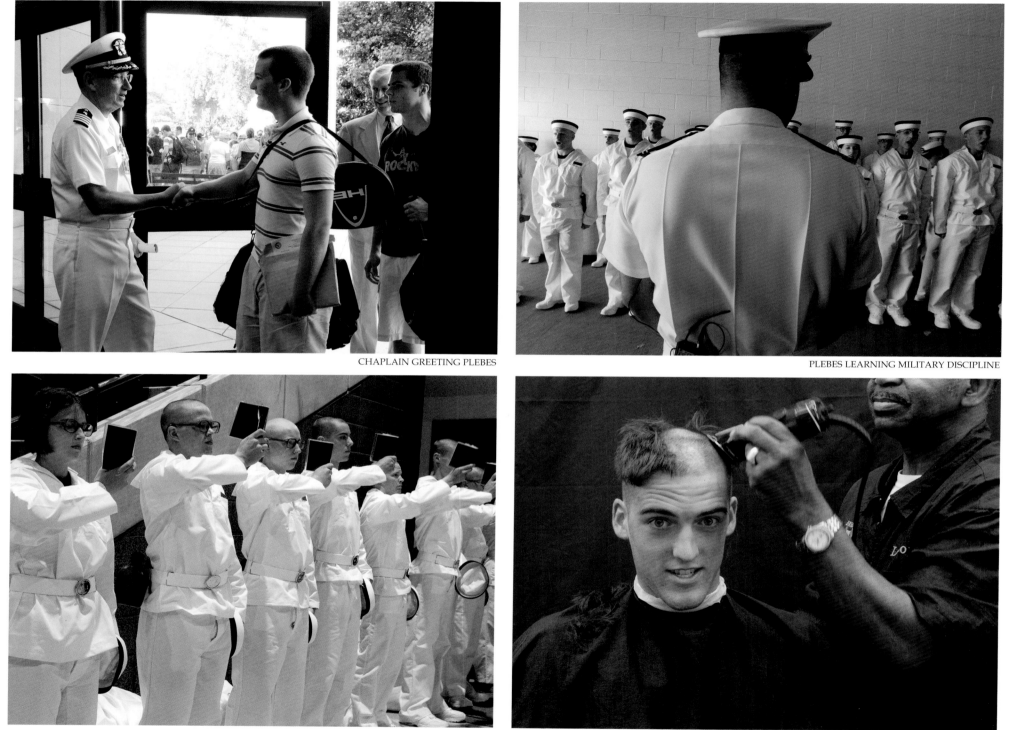

CHAPLAIN GREETING PLEBES

PLEBES LEARNING MILITARY DISCIPLINE

PLEBES READING *REEF POINTS*

PLEBE GETTING NEW HAIRCUT

PLEBE SUMMER begins with I-DAY (Induction-Day). Rather than an acceptance letter, these young students received a "permit to report" in late June. It is usually a hot summer day that changes life as he or she knows it. After a greeting by the chaplain, plebes receive their new uniforms and a haircut, and begin memorizing the plebe orientation manual, *Reef Points*.

UPPERCLASS DETAILERS

PLEBES TAKING OATH OF OFFICE

PLEBES WAITING TO TAKE OATH OF OFFICE

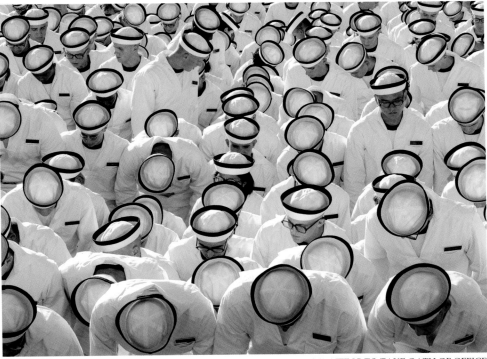

PLEBES WAITING TO TAKE OATH OF OFFICE

I-DAY ends with the ceremonial administration of the oath of office. The formal oath of office is signed earlier in the day. This is the point at which civilian teenagers are transformed into midshipmen. While other college students are still enjoying the beach, beer and fun, these plebes are led by seniors known as "detailers" who oversee a summer of challenging physical training and military discipline.

151

FULL DRESS BLUES

SERVICE DRESS WHITES

MIDSHIPMEN UNIFORMS   Unlike any other college, the midshipmen of the Naval Academy wear uniforms throughout the school year. These are two of the several different uniforms they wear depending on the time of year, the job they are performing or the occasion they are attending. Midshipmen reference the "Plan of the Day" to determine which uniform is prescribed for various events. Midshipmen are held to high standards regarding uniform wear and cleanliness. Violations may result in demerits.

SEA TRIALS At the end of "Plebe Year," the midshipmen participate in this test of strength, endurance and teamwork. The day starts shortly after midnight with physical challenges such as self-defense, obstacle courses and infantry squad scenarios. This marks the end of plebe year and the midshipmen now have the opportunity for more responsibility and privileges.

DEPARTMENT OF AEROSPACE ENGINEERING

DEPARTMENT OF NAVAL ARCHITECTURE AND OCEAN ENGINEERING

DEPARTMENT OF SEAMANSHIP AND NAVIGATION

DEPARTMENT OF POLITICAL SCIENCE

ACADEMIC STUDIES Most people are inspired by the midshipmen's uniforms and parades and are not as aware of the Naval Academy's high academic standards. The course of study is built around a Bachelor of Science degree. The Naval Academy usually ranks as one of the top engineering schools in the country.

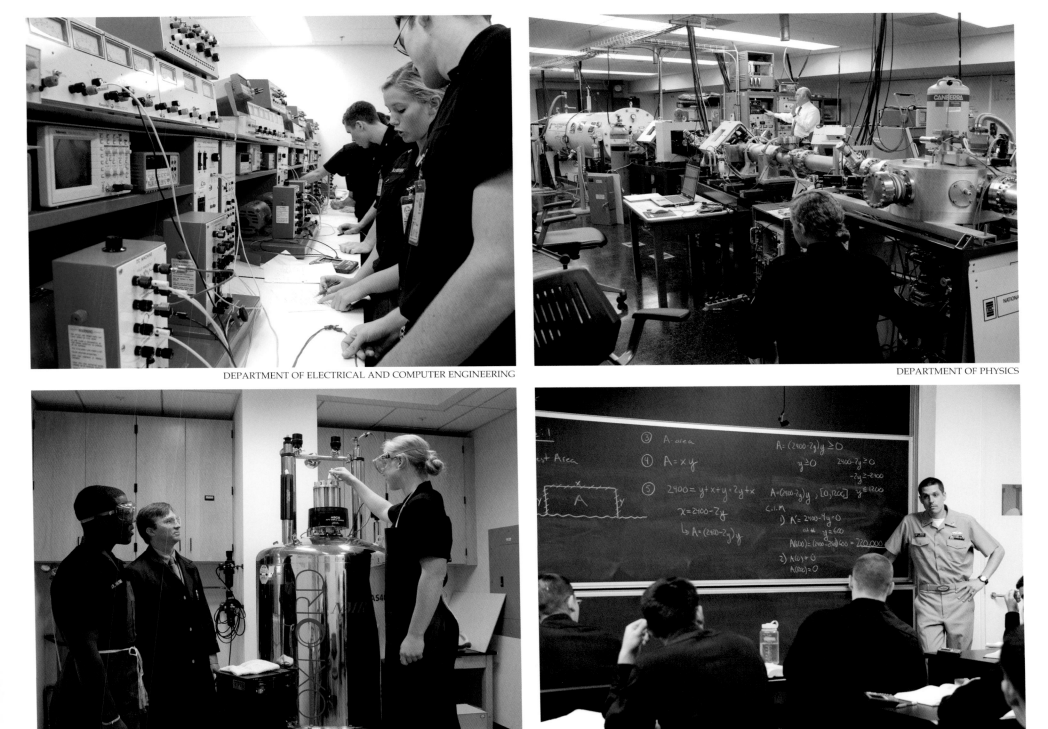

DEPARTMENT OF ELECTRICAL AND COMPUTER ENGINEERING

DEPARTMENT OF PHYSICS

DEPARTMENT OF CHEMISTRY

DEPARTMENT OF MATHEMATICS

ACADEMIC STUDIES The academics are divided into five divisions: Engineering and Weapons; Mathematics; Science; Humanities and Social Sciences; Professional Development and Officer Development. The faculty of 560 at the Academy is made up of both civilian and military personnel. The student/faculty ratio is 8:1 with class sizes ranging from 10 to 22.

ICE HOCKEY AT BRIGADE SPORTS COMPLEX

WOMEN'S TRACK AND FIELD

BRIGADE BOXING FINALS

WOMEN'S TRACK AND FIELD

ATHLETICS Just as the Academy promotes academic development; it is also a must for midshipmen to fulfill their requirement for physical development. Athletic teams are an integral part of the overall education. All midshipmen are required to participate in a varsity sport, an intramural sport or a club sport. Athletics provide leadership opportunities and the experiences of team play, cooperation, commitment and individual sacrifice. The primary goal of the physical education curriculum is fitness, which is vital for health, personal appearance and well-being of future naval officers.

WOMEN'S BASKETBALL

OFFSHORE SAILING

BASEBALL

OFFSHORE SAILING

ATHLETICS The Naval Academy has some of the finest gyms, pools and athletic facilities in the world: Halsey Field House; Lejeune Physical Education Center; MacDonough Hall; the Glenn Warner Soccer Facility; Rip Miller Field; the Robert Crown Sailing Center; the Wesley Brown Field House; the Brigade Sports Complex and the newly renovated Navy-Marine Corps Memorial Stadium – to name a few. In the 2006-2007 season, Naval Academy athletic teams had a record of 297 – 156 – 3 (.655).

NAVY-MARINE CORPS MEMORIAL STADIUM

BRIGADE ON THE FIELD AT NAVY-MARINE CORPS MEMORIAL STADIUM

BRIGADE ON THE FIELD AT NAVY-MARINE CORPS MEMORIAL STADIUM

NAVY-MARINE CORPS MEMORIAL STADIUM

HOME GAMES AT THE NAVY-MARINE CORPS MEMORIAL STADIUM are full of fanfare with a parade of the midshipmen onto the field to get things started. It's not unusual to see planes or helicopters flying over and sometimes parachutists from Navy and Marine Corps units parachuting into the stadium. The newly renovated stadium seats 34,000 midshipmen, alumni and other Navy fans.

ARMY NAVY GAME

BRIGADE ON THE FIELD AT THE ARMY NAVY GAME

ARMY NAVY GAME

PRESIDENT BUSH AT THE ARMY NAVY GAME

THE ARMY NAVY FOOTBALL GAME has become one of the nation's most spirited athletic rivalries. Both the Navy Midshipmen and the Army Cadets march into the stadium and stand in formation on the field before taking their seats. If the President of the United States attends, he routinely sits on one side for half of the game and on the other side for the other half of the game. Navy has a record 13 straight wins over its rival service academies.

SURFACE VESSEL TRAINING AT MAYPORT, FL

SUBMARINE TRAINING AT MAYPORT, FL

MARINE CORPS HELICOPTER TRAINING AT MCAS NEW RIVER, NC

NAVAL ASSAULT TRAINING AT NAB LITTLE CREEK, VA

PRO TRA MID is Summer Training at the end of the midshipmen's second year at the Naval Academy. It serves as an introduction to all of the career options they will have available in the Navy or Marine Corps once they graduate. For six weeks, they rotate from training aboard surface vessels and submarines to helicopters and Marine assault vehicles.

MARINE CORPS TRAINING IN THE MOUT AT CAMP LEJEUNE, NC

NAVY AIRCRAFT F/A-18E AT NAS OCEANA, VA

MARINE CORPS TRAINING AT CAMP LEJEUNE, NC

MARINE CORPS TRAINING AT CAMP LEJEUNE, NC

PRO TRA MID continues at Camp Lejeune where midshipmen in combat gear experience a simulated fire fight at the MOUT with 9mm paint balls. They are introduced to amphibious assault vehicles (AAV's), Abrams M1-A1 tanks, and naval fixed-wing aircraft. This provides midshipmen with a well-rounded training opportunity and further prepares them for service in the Navy or Marine Corps.

HERNDON MONUMENT CLIMB

COLOR PARADE

HERNDON MONUMENT CLIMB

COLOR PARADE

COMMISSIONING WEEK is a week of parades and activities leading up to Naval Academy graduation. As one class of midshipmen prepares to graduate, the other classes have a series of traditional transitions they make to claim the next class level. Plebes climb the Herndon Monument and replace the plebe hat with a midshipmen's hat to signify the end of their first year.

COMPANY COMMANDERS GO IN THE FOUNTAIN AFTER COLOR PARADE

RING DANCE

COMPANY COMMANDERS GO IN THE FOUNTAIN AFTER COLOR PARADE

RING DANCE

COMMISSIONING WEEK The Color Parade is the last parade for graduating seniors. As part of a tradition, at the end of the parade, the plebes throw their upperclass company commanders into the fountain. The uniform seniors have been wearing will now be replaced with a Navy or Marine uniform. **THE RING DANCE** takes place at the end of junior year when the juniors receive their class rings and make the transition toward senior status.

BLUE ANGELS FLYOVER

PRESIDENT OBAMA ADDRESSES THE GRADUATING MIDSHIPMEN

OATH OF OFFICE

GRADUATES DISPLAY THEIR DEGREES AND COMMISSIONS AS OFFICERS

GRADUATION DAY is the ending of the four-year mental and physical challenge the midshipmen have endured. As with any graduation, there are speeches and the awarding of degrees. In addition, at the Naval Academy, the graduates receive their commissions into the Navy or Marine Corps and take the ceremonial oath of office. As part of the tradition, the Blue Angles fly over the stadium in perfect formation.

HAT TOSS

GRADUATION DAY The traditional "hat toss" is the release of the old midshipmen's hat into the air. The newly commissioned naval officers will now proudly wear their new officer's hats. The Naval Academy has a record of 100% employment for graduates. Each graduate will be deployed as an officer in the Navy or Marine Corps for at least five years of service.

MELGES 24 NORTH AMERICAN CHAMPIONSHIP These Melges 24 competitors are running with the wind as they head to the next point of the course. Hosted by the Eastport Yacht Club, this is one of the most prestigious sailboat races in the world. Sailing champions come from all over the world to participate in this race.

DIRECTORY

THE ANNAPOLIS INN
144 Prince George Street
Annapolis, MD 21401
410-295-5200
www.annapolisinn.com

ANNAPOLIS OPERA, INC.
801 Chase Street Suite 304
Annapolis, MD 21401
410-267-8135
www.annapolisopera.org

ANNAPOLIS SYMPHONY ORCHESTRA
801 Chase Street
Annapolis, MD 21401
410-269-1132
www.annapolissymphony.org

ANNAPOLIS TOWNE CENTRE
1906 Towne Centre Blvd., Suite 143
Annapolis, MD 21401
410-573-9050
www.visitatc.com

ANNAPOLIS YACHT CLUB
2 Compromise Street
Annapolis, MD 21401
410-263-9279
www.annapolisyc.org

BALLET THEATRE OF MARYLAND
801 Chase Street
Annapolis, MD 21401
410-263-8289
www.balletmaryland.org

BOATYARD BAR & GRILL
400 Fourth Street
Annapolis, MD 21403
410-216-6206
www.boatyardbarandgrill.com

BUDDY'S CRABS & RIBS
100 Main Street
Annapolis, MD 21401
410-626-1100/410-269-1800/301-261-2500
www.buddysonline.com

CANTLER'S RIVERSIDE INN
458 Forest Beach Road
Annapolis, MD 21401
410-757-1311
www.cantlers.com

CAROLINE'S CAKES
1580 Whitehall Road
Annapolis, MD 21409
410-349-2212
888-801-2253 (CAKE)
www.carolinescakes.com

CHESAPEAKE LIGHT CRAFT
1805 George Avenue
Annapolis, MD 21401
410-267-0137
www.clcboats.com

CHICK & RUTH'S DELLY
165 Main Street
Annapolis, MD 21401
410-269-6737
www.chickandruths.com
www.scotlaurinn.com
www.facesofvalorusa.com

EASTPORT YACHT CLUB
317 First Street
Annapolis, MD 21403
410-267-9549
www.eastportyc.org

FEDERAL HOUSE BAR & GRILLE
22-24 Market Space
Annapolis, MD 21401
410-268-2576
www.federalhouserestaurant.com

GIBSON'S LODGINGS BED & BREAKFAST INN
110 Prince George Street
Annapolis, MD 21401
410-268-5555 / 877-330-0057
www.gibsonslodgings.com

GOVERNOR MARTIN O'MALLEY
100 State Circle
Annapolis, MD 21401
410-974-3901
www.governor.maryland.gov

JAGUAR LAND ROVER ANNAPOLIS
101 Ferguson Road
Annapolis, MD 21409
410-349-8090
www.jlra.net

JOBSON SAILING, INC.
3 Church Circle
Annapolis, MD 21401
410-263-4630
www.jobsonsailing.com

LIVE ARTS MARYLAND
801 Chase Street
Annapolis, MD 21401
410-263-1906
www.annapolischorale.org

LOEWS ANNAPOLIS HOTEL
126 West Street
Annapolis, MD 21401
410-263-7777
www.loewsannapolis.com

MARYLAND HALL FOR THE CREATIVE ARTS
801 Chase Street
Annapolis, MD 21401
410-263-5544/410-280-5640 (box office)
www.marylandhall.org

MARYLAND RENAISSANCE FESTIVAL
P.O.Box 315
Crownsville, MD 21032
Located off Crownsville Road
410-266-7304/800-296-7304
www.rennfest.com
www.marylandrenaissancefestival.com

NATIONAL SAILING HALL OF FAME
& SAILING CENTER
67-69 Prince George Street
Annapolis, MD 21401
410-295-3022
www.nshof.org

THE O'CALLAGHAN ANNAPOLIS HOTEL
174 West Street
Annapolis, MD 21401
410-263-7700
www.ocallaghanhotels.com

PARK PLACE
5 Park Place
Annapolis, MD 21401
410-216-9267
www.distinctlyannapolis.com

PERFORMANCE CRUISING
7364 Edgewood Road
Annapolis, MD 21403
410-626-2720
www.performancecruising.com

RAMS HEAD ON STAGE
RAMS HEAD TAVERN
33 West Street
Annapolis, MD 21401
410-268-4545
www.ramsheadonstage.com
www.ramsheadtavern.com

SHERATON ANNAPOLIS HOTEL
173 Jennifer Road
Annapolis, MD 21401
410-266-3131
www.sheraton.com/annapolis

SOUTH RIVER BOAT RENTALS
2802 Solomons Island Road
Edgewater, MD 21037
410-956-9729
www.southriverboatrentals.com

THE WESTIN ANNAPOLIS
100 Westgate Circle
Annapolis, MD 21401
410-972-4315
www.westin.com/annapolis

UNITED STATES NAVAL ACADEMY
Armel-Leftwich Visitors' Center
U.S. Naval Academy
Annapolis, MD 21402
410-293-8687 (TOUR)
410-293-4438 (GIFT)
www.usna.edu/visit.htm

YELLOWFIN STEAK & FISH HOUSE
2840 Solomons Island Road
Edgewater, MD 21037
410-573-1333
www.yellowfinrestaurant.com

WEDNESDAY NIGHT RACES This is a critical point of the Wednesday night race course depending on how the wind is blowing. Returning back from the Chesapeake Bay these sailboats are in the process of taking down their spinnakers and putting up their jibs so than can tack to the finish line at the Annapolis Yacht Club.

IF YOU WOULD LIKE TO HAVE ANY OF THE PHOTOS IN THIS BOOK FOR YOUR HOME OR OFFICE THEY ARE ALL AVAILABLE IN PRINTS FROM 5" X 7" TO 8' X 16' FROM ROGER MILLER SEE rogermillerphoto.com.